When You're AuDHD and Your Child Has PDA

A Practical Survival Guide for Neurodivergent Parents Raising Demand-Avoidant Children

The AuDHD Family Series — Book 1

Ruth Margie Holmes

First Edition:2026

ISBN: 9781764563741

Table of Contents

Preface

The parenting advice that fills shelves, feeds social media algorithms, and circulates in pediatrician waiting rooms was built on a single assumption: that the parent reading it has a nervous system that processes demands, recovers from stress, and sustains routine in broadly neurotypical ways. Remove that assumption and most of the advice not only stops working. It actively produces worse outcomes.

There is a growing population of adults who received their autism or ADHD diagnosis late, sometimes in their thirties or forties, sometimes in direct response to their child being assessed first. Among those parents, a significant proportion are raising children whose profiles include demand avoidance, sometimes formally diagnosed as Pathological Demand Avoidance, sometimes described in other clinical language, but recognizable in its core features: a nervous system that experiences imposed demands as threat, that resists compliance not out of defiance but out of genuine neurological necessity. The combination of a late-diagnosed AuDHD parent and a demand-avoidant child produces a household that no existing parenting guide was designed to address.

The current literature on PDA parenting is increasingly strong. Research on low-demand approaches, declarative language, and autonomy-supportive environments has produced genuinely useful frameworks. But that literature assumes a neurotypical adult on the delivering end of the strategies, someone whose executive function is intact under pressure, whose nervous system recovers quickly from high-intensity interactions, and whose sensory environment is not itself a source of daily difficulty. For the AuDHD parent, these assumptions hollow out the advice at the moment it is most needed.

What has been missing is a guide that holds both sides of the dynamic simultaneously. Not a book about PDA with a chapter acknowledging that parents get tired, and not a book about AuDHD parenting that treats the child's profile as background context. A guide that treats the double-ND household as its actual subject, with the specific collision of two neurodivergent nervous systems as the central problem to be understood and addressed.

The framework in these pages draws on polyvagal theory, research on autistic burnout, ADHD executive function literature, the double empathy problem, PDA-specific parenting studies, and the growing body of work on late-diagnosed adults navigating identity and intergenerational neurodivergence. It also draws on something that research alone cannot supply: the specific quality of understanding that comes from demand avoidance being a lived experience rather than a theoretical one. The AuDHD parent reading about PDA is not reading from the outside. They are reading about something they have felt. That is not a small thing, and this guide treats it as the advantage it actually is.

The household being described here is real, it is specific, and it has been underserved for long enough.

Introduction I Think We're Both Neurodivergent

What Late Discovery Actually Looks Like

Most parents who pick up this book are not starting from zero. They have already spent months, maybe years, piecing together information about Pathological Demand Avoidance. They have read the articles. They have joined the Facebook groups at midnight. They have printed out checklists and carried them to appointments, hoping someone would finally take them seriously.

And somewhere in the middle of all that research, something happened. A description of PDA turned up in a book, or a thread, or a Reddit post. And it did not just describe their child. It described them.

That moment has a particular quality to it. It is quiet. A little disorienting. And underneath the confusion, there is often something that feels uncomfortably like relief.

If you found yourself in that moment, this book was written with you in mind. You are parenting a child who is demand-avoidant while carrying a brain that processes the world through the combined lens of autism and ADHD. That is a specific experience. It creates specific challenges, specific blind spots, and specific advantages that no other kind of parent can claim.

This introduction is not here to promise that things will get easier the moment you finish reading it. But it will help you understand exactly what you are dealing with, why you are dealing with it, and how to use this book in a way that actually works for your brain.

Why It Runs in Families

Autism is one of the most heritable conditions studied in human genetics research. A meta-analysis published in the Journal of Child Psychology and Psychiatry, which reviewed data from 37 twin studies, found that the heritability of autism spectrum disorder ranges from 64 to 91 percent (Tick et al., 2016). That figure is not surprising to most parents who are themselves autistic. They did not need a study to tell them their child got it from somewhere.

ADHD follows a similar pattern. The World Federation of ADHD International Consensus Statement, which reviewed over 3,000 studies, confirmed heritability rates of approximately 74 percent, placing ADHD among the most heritable conditions in all of psychiatry (Faraone et al., 2021).

When autism and ADHD occur together, researchers refer to this co-occurrence by a number of terms, though the word AuDHD has become widely used in community spaces. Research published in the journal Autism found that autistic people with co-occurring ADHD described a lifetime of having their struggles fall between two diagnostic categories, leaving them without clear support from either direction (Leedham et al., 2020). Many AuDHD people reach adulthood without a full picture of what is happening in their brain because each condition can partially mask the other during assessment.

PDA sits within the autism spectrum and, like autism itself, tends to show up across generations. Parents who discover their child's PDA profile often find themselves reading descriptions that match not just their child's behavior, but their own internal experience of the world. The demand sensitivity. The fierce need for autonomy. The way certain kinds of pressure feel physically unbearable, like something is closing in.

This is not a coincidence. It is biology. And recognizing it is not a detour from understanding your child. It is the beginning of understanding both of you.

Here is what this looked like for one parent:

Consider Elowen (name changed), a woman in her late thirties who brought her eight-year-old daughter to a PDA specialist after two years of school-related breakdowns. During the assessment process, the specialist handed Elowen a checklist used to screen for pathological demand avoidance in children. Elowen read through the items. Her daughter ticked most of them. But as she read, she kept pausing. The way demands felt physically threatening. The need to control her own time and choices. The way she had learned, over decades, to hide how much everyday pressure cost her. She ticked most of those boxes too. On the drive home, Elowen said nothing for a long time. Then she told her partner: "I think I've been masking for thirty-eight years." What followed was not a quick or tidy process. Elowen pursued her own assessment, received an AuDHD diagnosis at thirty-nine, and spent several months processing what that meant. She describes the experience now as clarifying rather than comforting. Things that had never made sense before, including her struggles with work, relationships, sensory overwhelm, and the way certain social situations left her wrecked for days, started to fit into a different picture. Parenting her daughter did not get easier overnight. But understanding her own nervous system changed how she approached her daughter's. She stopped trying to be a neurotypical parent and started figuring out what kind of parent her actual brain could be.

When Two Neurotypes Live Together

AuDHD is not simply autism plus ADHD. The two neurotypes interact in ways that create a profile that can look different from either one on its own. Autistic traits can mask ADHD symptoms, and ADHD traits can mask autistic ones. This is part of why so many AuDHD people reach adulthood without a clear diagnosis, or with only one of the two identified (Leedham et al., 2020).

In the context of parenting a PDA child, both neurotypes become relevant at the same time, in the same space, day after day. The autistic parent may find their child's meltdowns physically overwhelming because of their own sensory sensitivity. The ADHD parent may find it genuinely hard to maintain the kind of consistent, low-demand approach that PDA parenting requires. The AuDHD parent experiences both of those things at once.

And there is another layer. Many AuDHD adults grew up without support. They adapted to a world that did not account for them by developing strategies that worked, at least some of the time, but that came at a cost. Masking. Hypervigilance. A constant background sense of effort that other people did not seem to feel. Some of those adaptations become obstacles when you are trying to parent a child whose nervous system works like yours does. You know what demand avoidance feels like from the inside. That is an asset. But it can also mean that your child's behavior lands differently for you than it would for a neurotypical parent. It can activate your own stress response faster. It can trigger your own sense of failure when things go wrong.

The strategies in this book are written with that in mind. They do not ask you to become a different kind of person. They work with the brain you have.

Here is how one father described his first year after dual diagnosis:

Consider Aldwyn (name changed), who was diagnosed with ADHD at thirty-four, after his son received an autism assessment at age six. His son's diagnosis prompted Aldwyn's wife to ask a question they had both been circling around for years: had anyone ever looked at Aldwyn? He had always been described as creative, scattered, and exhausting to be around. He had also been, since childhood, quietly overwhelmed in ways he could not explain. Noise. Texture. The accumulation of small undone tasks that other people seemed to carry without noticing. When Aldwyn's assessment came back, it included both ADHD and autism. The ADHD had been visible his whole life, in ways that got him labeled difficult and disruptive. The autism had hidden underneath, showing up mostly as exhaustion, sensory withdrawal, and a fierce need for things to go a particular way. His son, as it turned out, had a PDA profile. Aldwyn spent the first year after both diagnoses feeling like he was learning two languages at the same time: his own brain and his son's. What he found, slowly, was that some of what he understood about himself was directly useful. He knew what it felt like when a demand landed wrong. He knew the difference between choosing to do something and being told to do it. He did not always know what to do with that knowledge in the moment. But it gave him a starting point that no parenting book had ever offered him before.

What PDA Does to a Family

Pathological Demand Avoidance is best understood not as a behavioral problem but as an anxiety-driven profile of autism in which the nervous system perceives everyday demands as threats. The response to those perceived threats includes avoidance, negotiation, meltdowns, shutdowns, and what can look to the outside world like extreme oppositionality (O'Nions et al., 2014).

Standard parenting strategies do not work for PDA children. Reward charts, consequences, and structured routines can actively make things worse because they add more demands to an environment that already feels unsafe. What tends to help instead is a low-demand approach: reducing expectations, offering genuine choice, sharing control, and prioritizing the child's felt sense of safety over behavioral compliance.

For an AuDHD parent, putting a low-demand approach into practice has its own complications. It requires staying calm in the face of chaos when your own nervous system is already stretched. It requires indirect communication when your brain wants to be direct. It requires flexibility on the days when executive function is barely getting the household running. It requires repair after the moments when you could not hold it together, without drowning in shame about those moments.

None of that is impossible. But it looks different for you than it does for a neurotypical parent reading the same PDA parenting guide. This book is written for the version of it that is yours.

How to Read This Book

This book is built for executive-dysfunction-friendly brains. That means a few practical things.

You do not have to read it front to back. Each chapter is written to stand on its own. If Chapter 6.0 on school advocacy is the crisis you are dealing with right now, go there first. Come back to Chapter 2.0 on your nervous system when you have more space. The book will still make sense.

Chapters are broken into short sections with clear subheadings so it is easier to pick up and put down without losing your place entirely. If you have read a section before and forgotten it, that is fine. Reading it again is the system working as intended.

The practical prompts scattered through each chapter are not homework. You do not have to sit down and answer them in order. Some people find it useful to write the answers. Some find it more useful to sit with a question while they are making coffee or driving somewhere. Either way works.

The stories in each chapter are based on real situations, though names and identifying details have been changed. They are there to show that the things described in these pages happen to real people in real households, not just in clinical descriptions.

Here is how one parent made this work for him:

Consider Bramwell (name changed), who bought four different books about PDA before opening this one. He read the first three chapters of one, the last chapter of another, and spent a significant amount of time on a single paragraph in a third before putting it down and going to make tea. That is not a criticism of those books. It is a description of how his brain works when it is overloaded and looking for something specific. He did not want the full clinical history of pathological demand avoidance. He wanted to know what to do tonight, when his daughter refused to come to the table for dinner and things were about to escalate. He uses this book in ten-to-fifteen-minute chunks. He goes to the subheading that matches the problem he is currently in. He sometimes reads the same section three times in a week because he forgot he had already read it. That is fine. That is one of the reasons this book is structured the way it is.

What This Book Is Not

This book is not a clinical manual. It does not replace a therapist, a PDA specialist, or a pediatric psychiatrist. If you or your child are in crisis, please reach out to a professional who can give real-time, individualized support.

This book is also not a promise that applying these ideas will fix things. PDA parenting is not a problem you solve and move on from. It is an ongoing, shifting, genuinely demanding relationship that changes as your child grows and as you do. What this book aims to do is give you a clearer picture of what you are working with, and better tools for the days when it feels like too much.

And it does not assume a particular family structure, income level, or access to professional support. Some of what is described here will apply directly to your situation. Some will need adapting. Take what is useful and set aside what is not. There is no test at the end.

What Lies Ahead

The chapters that follow move through the territory of AuDHD parenting and PDA in a deliberate sequence, though as mentioned, you can read them in whatever order makes sense for where you are right now.

Chapter 1.0 looks at what it actually means to be a double neurodivergent household, and why the particular combination of AuDHD and PDA creates dynamics that no other parenting situation quite replicates.

Chapter 2.0 starts with you, because it has to. The way your nervous system is functioning right now determines how much capacity you have for your child. That is not a selfish starting point. It is how co-regulation works.

From there, the book moves through low-demand parenting adapted for AuDHD brains, the cascade effect of dual meltdowns, communication between neurodivergent brains, school advocacy, daily life and routines, your own late diagnosis and identity, co-parenting, burnout, and finally, the real advantages that come with being the specific kind of parent you are.

By the end, the aim is not that you have all the answers. It is that things that felt confusing feel clearer. And that you have a better sense of how to show up for your child with the brain you actually have, not the brain you think you should have.

What This Means

This introduction has covered three ideas that shape everything in the chapters ahead.

First, if you are AuDHD and your child has a PDA profile, the overlap between your neurotype and theirs is not random. Autism and ADHD are highly heritable, and PDA as an autism profile follows the same genetic pattern. The mirror moment that many parents describe, of seeing themselves in their child's assessment, is grounded in real neurology.

Second, being an AuDHD parent of a PDA child is a specific experience. The strategies in this book are built to account for how your brain actually works, including the parts that make standard parenting advice fall flat.

Third, this book is meant to be used in whatever way fits your brain. Non-linear. Chunked. Returned to as needed. There is no right way.

Take a breath. Then turn to whatever chapter calls to you first.

Chapter 1.0 Understanding the Double ND Household

Two Neurotypes One Roof

There is a particular kind of household that most parenting books have never tried to describe. It is the one where the child is demand-avoidant and the parent is also neurodivergent. Where the child's meltdown is loud and physical and consuming, and the parent standing in the hallway is not unmoved by it. They are not calmly riding it out. They are flooded. Their own nervous system has picked up the distress signal and responded in kind.

This is the double neurodivergent household. And if you are reading this, there is a reasonable chance you live in one.

The term double neurodivergent household is not a clinical label. It is simply a description of what happens when a parent who is AuDHD raises a child with a PDA profile. Both people in that dynamic process the world through nervous systems that respond differently from the neurotypical baseline. Both have genuine needs that can come into direct conflict with each other. And both bring real strengths that no other parent-child combination can quite replicate.

Understanding how that works, in both directions, is the foundation for everything else in this book.

What AuDHD Looks Like Day to Day

Before looking at what happens when AuDHD meets PDA, it helps to be clear about what AuDHD actually involves in daily life.

Autism and ADHD are both neurodevelopmental conditions affecting how the brain processes information, regulates attention, and responds to sensory input and social demands. When they occur together, which happens more often than was previously recognized, the result is not simply a combination of the two sets of traits. The neurotypes interact. Research published in the journal Frontiers in Psychiatry found that adults with co-occurring autism and ADHD reported greater functional difficulties and lower quality of life than those with either condition alone, partly because the combined profile creates patterns that standard supports for each individual condition do not address (Antshel et al., 2013).

In practical terms, this interaction shows up in a few recurring ways. The autistic drive for routine and predictability can clash with the ADHD tendency toward novelty-seeking and impulsivity. The autistic preference for clear, direct communication can conflict with the ADHD pattern of speaking before thinking. The autistic need for low-sensory environments can coexist with the ADHD need for stimulation. These internal tensions do not go away just because you are an adult and a parent. They continue, and they affect how you respond to your child's needs minute by minute.

A typical morning in a double-ND household might involve a parent who has already spent forty minutes managing their own sensory overload from noise, light, and the texture of clothing, while simultaneously trying to reduce demands on a child who has refused to engage with any part of the morning routine. By nine in the morning, both people may already be at or near their capacity.

When Sensory Needs Collide

Sensory processing differences are one of the most concrete and under-discussed aspects of the double-ND household. Autistic sensory profiles often include both hypersensitivity (finding certain sounds, textures, or lights acutely uncomfortable) and hyposensitivity (needing more input in other areas to feel regulated). ADHD adds its own sensory dimension, with many ADHDers finding that background noise and environmental chaos either overwhelm them or, paradoxically, are the condition under which they function best.

PDA children tend to have significant sensory sensitivities of their own, often linked to the heightened anxiety that characterizes their profile. A PDA child in meltdown is typically producing high volumes of distress, physically and verbally. For a neurotypical parent, this is hard. For an autistic parent with auditory sensitivity, it can be physically painful. The noise is not just loud. It is the specific kind of sensory input that their nervous system has the least tolerance for.

Research in the area of parental stress and sensory processing found that parents who are themselves sensory-sensitive experience significantly higher stress responses to their children's emotional dysregulation than parents without sensory differences (Parham & Ecker, 2007). This is not a failure of parenting. It is a physiological response. The parent's nervous system is responding to threat signals exactly as it was built to respond.

The problem, of course, is that at the moment when a PDA child is in meltdown and most needs a calm, regulated adult presence, the AuDHD parent may be least able to provide it. This is the sensory collision. It is real, it is common in double-ND households, and ignoring it does not make it smaller.

What does help is naming it, planning for it, and building in strategies that account for it. Chapter 4.0 goes into the cascade effect in detail and offers specific tools for dual-dysregulation moments. For now, the important thing is to understand that sensory collision in the double-ND household is a structural feature, not a personal failure.

Consider Crispin (name changed), a father in his early forties who spent three years believing he was simply too anxious to parent his daughter through her meltdowns. Every time she escalated, he felt something close to panic. His hearing would sharpen. His chest would tighten. He would walk out of the room, not because he was abandoning her, but because remaining in the room felt physically impossible. He described it later as being caught in two storms at once. His daughter's external storm and his own internal one. When Crispin received his autism assessment at forty-two, the sensory component of his profile was immediately obvious to the assessing clinician. His auditory sensitivity registered at clinical levels. He had not been failing to parent through difficulty. He had been parenting through a physiological response that he had never been given the language to describe. Once he had that language, he could start to plan around it. Not by disappearing from the room, but by identifying the point just before his own flooding and building in a short, deliberate pause that allowed him to return regulated enough to be useful.

Demand Avoidance Meets Executive Dysfunction

The second major collision in the double-ND household is less visible than the sensory one but equally significant. PDA is driven by an anxiety response to demands. The PDA child's nervous system reads demands, including gentle ones, including ones framed as choices, as threats to autonomy and safety. The more demands are pressed, the more the child resists, often in ways that look deliberate but are primarily driven by neurological threat response.

ADHD executive dysfunction means that the AuDHD parent often struggles with consistency, follow-through, planning, and initiating tasks. The low-demand approach that works best for PDA children requires the parent to be thoughtful, flexible, and patient about how they present requests. It requires not defaulting to direct demands under pressure. It requires remembering to frame things indirectly even when tired, distracted, or overwhelmed.

This is genuinely hard when executive function is compromised. The ADHD brain under stress is more likely to revert to direct, urgent communication, exactly the kind that activates a PDA child's threat response most intensely. It is not a character flaw. It is how executive dysfunction behaves when the cognitive load is high.

Research on executive function in ADHD has shown that working memory, the ability to hold and use information in the moment, is among the most consistently impaired functions in ADHD adults (Barkley, 1997). Low-demand parenting requires the parent to hold in mind, simultaneously, how to frame a request, what their child's current state is, what has worked before, and what might escalate things. That is a significant working memory load for any parent. For an ADHD parent already managing their own sensory input and stress, it can be genuinely overloading.

Again, this does not mean low-demand parenting is impossible for the AuDHD parent. It means it needs to be supported differently. Scripts help. Written reminders help. Pre-planning the most common demand-heavy moments helps. The specifics are covered in Chapter 3.0 and Chapter 5.0. The point here is to understand why this particular collision happens, so you stop attributing it to things like lack of effort or insufficient love for your child.

Consider Fenwick (name changed), whose son has a confirmed PDA profile and who received an ADHD diagnosis eighteen months after his son's. Fenwick described the early years of parenting his son as a series of interactions he could replay clearly but could not, at the time, understand why they had gone wrong. He would ask his son to put his shoes on. His son would refuse. Fenwick would repeat the request, more firmly. His son would escalate. Fenwick, now also escalating, would issue a direct instruction. His son would melt down. What Fenwick could not see in those moments was that each step of that sequence was the predictable output of two different neurological systems interacting badly. His ADHD brain defaulted to direct and repetitive under pressure. His son's PDA profile escalated in direct proportion to the demand intensity. Neither of them was choosing to make it worse. Both of them were doing what their nervous systems were built to do.

The Strength in This Combination

This chapter has spent time on the difficulties, and they are real. But the double-ND household also carries genuine advantages, and they are worth taking seriously rather than dismissing as consolation.

The most significant advantage is one that no neurotypical parent can fully access. AuDHD parents know, from the inside, what demand avoidance feels like. They know what it is to have a task feel impossible not because of difficulty or laziness but because something about the demand itself lands as threat. They know what it is to need control over how something happens, not just whether it happens. They know what it is to be overwhelmed by something that most people around them seem to manage easily.

That lived knowledge is not just empathy. It is information. It gives the AuDHD parent a kind of interpretive access to their child's experience that goes beyond anything a book or course can provide. When their child refuses to engage with something, the AuDHD parent is more likely to read that refusal accurately. Not as defiance. Not as manipulation. As a nervous system doing what nervous systems do when they are under threat.

Research on parental empathy and its effects on child outcomes has consistently shown that accurate parental interpretation of child behavior, sometimes called mind-mindedness, significantly predicts better outcomes for children in terms of emotional regulation and attachment security (Meins et al., 2001). The AuDHD parent who understands their child's refusal as anxiety rather than opposition is, in that moment, demonstrating exactly this kind of accurate interpretation. And that matters enormously for the child's experience of being parented.

Pattern recognition is the second strength. Many autistic people have a highly developed capacity for identifying patterns, including patterns in their child's behavior that less observant parents might miss. The quiet signs of an approaching meltdown. The specific demands that reliably cause escalation versus the ones that can be navigated. The time of day, the sensory conditions, the preceding interactions that create the conditions for a crisis. Autistic parents often notice these patterns early and with accuracy.

The third strength is in creative problem-solving. ADHD brains often generate novel approaches quickly, and where standard methods fail, as they reliably do with PDA children, the capacity to generate alternatives is a meaningful asset. The parent who can think laterally, reframe requests creatively, and generate options in the moment has a genuine advantage in low-demand parenting.

Consider Hadrian (name changed), whose daughter was diagnosed with a PDA profile at age seven. Hadrian himself carries both autism and ADHD diagnoses, received in his mid-thirties. He describes his approach to parenting his daughter as built almost entirely on pattern recognition. He keeps a simple log, not because any professional told him to, but because his brain naturally started tracking what preceded the hard days and what preceded the easier ones. Over eight months he identified that his daughter's most consistent crisis days followed evenings with more than one transition, regardless of how low-demand the transitions themselves were. That observation, which most parents would not have noticed or tracked, allowed him to reduce crisis frequency significantly by protecting her evenings from multiple transitions. No therapist gave him that information. He found it through the same pattern-recognition tendency that had, for most of his life, been described to him only as a quirk or a fixation.

What Your Child Sees in You

There is one more thing worth saying in this chapter, and it matters more than it might initially appear.

Your child, if they are old enough to notice, sees a parent who is also neurodivergent. They see an adult who sometimes gets overwhelmed. An adult who finds certain things hard. An adult who does not always manage to be calm and consistent and perfect. And they also see an adult who is still there. Still trying. Still working to understand them.

For a PDA child, who has very likely already experienced significant misattunement from neurotypical adults who could not understand why their approach was failing, seeing a parent who genuinely gets it from the inside is not a small thing. It is, potentially, the most stabilizing thing in their world.

That is not a reason to pretend the hard parts are not hard. It is a reason to take seriously the unique position you are in.

Key Takeaways

The double neurodivergent household is shaped by the interaction of AuDHD in the parent and PDA in the child. Two real collision points define this dynamic: sensory needs that activate each other under stress, and the combination of demand avoidance in the child with executive dysfunction in the parent.

Neither collision is a personal failing. Both are the predictable output of two neurodivergent nervous systems sharing the same space.

The strengths in this combination are equally real. Lived empathy for demand avoidance, accurate pattern recognition, and lateral problem-solving are all assets that the AuDHD parent brings to PDA parenting in ways no neurotypical parent can replicate.

And underneath all of it, your child has a parent who understands from the inside what their nervous system is doing. That understanding, built on and applied consistently, is the most useful thing you can offer.

Chapter 2.0 Your Nervous System Is the Foundation

Why Your State Matters First

Every piece of advice about PDA parenting eventually arrives at the same place. The child needs to feel safe. Safety is communicated through the parent's presence, tone, and state. And the parent's state, in a double neurodivergent household, is not something that can be managed by deciding to be calm.

This chapter starts with you. Not because your needs are more important than your child's. Because the nervous system does not work in a way that allows you to give what you do not have. Co-regulation, the process by which a regulated adult helps a dysregulated child return to a manageable state, is not possible if the adult is themselves dysregulated. This is not a moral position. It is neuroscience.

So before anything else, this chapter is about your nervous system. What it is doing. Why it matters. And what you can actually do about it, with an AuDHD brain, in a household that runs at a consistently high level of demand.

How the Nervous System Works

The autonomic nervous system governs the body's responses to the environment. Stephen Porges' Polyvagal Theory, first published in 1994 and refined significantly since, offers one of the most practically useful ways to understand how this system works, especially in the context of parenting and co-regulation (Porges, 2011).

The theory describes three main states. The first is the ventral vagal state, which corresponds to a sense of safety, connection, and calm engagement. In this state, a person can think clearly, respond flexibly, and connect with others. This is the state from which effective parenting is possible.

The second is the sympathetic activation state, the familiar fight-or-flight response. Heart rate increases. Attention narrows. The body prepares to deal with a perceived threat. In mild forms, this state produces anxiety, irritability, and urgency. In stronger forms, it produces panic, rage, or impulsive action.

The third is the dorsal vagal state, sometimes called shutdown or freeze. This is the body's last-resort response to overwhelming threat. It produces disconnection, emotional numbness, exhaustion, and withdrawal. Many autistic people recognize this as what happens after extended sensory or social overload.

In the double-ND household, all three of these states can cycle through a single morning. The parent may start in a reasonable ventral vagal state, shift to sympathetic activation when their child begins escalating, and move toward dorsal vagal shutdown if the escalation continues long enough. Meanwhile, their child is running their own version of exactly this sequence.

The AuDHD Nervous System Specifically

For AuDHD adults, the autonomic nervous system has some specific characteristics that affect how these states are reached and how long they last.

Autistic people tend to spend less time in the ventral vagal zone and more time in low-level sympathetic activation, even in environments that appear calm to others (Bal et al., 2010). Sensory input that other people filter out, background noise, flickering lights, fabric textures, the ambient sounds of a household in the morning, can keep the autistic nervous system in a low-level alert state. This means the autistic parent is often already closer to their threshold when a crisis begins.

ADHD adds an additional layer. The ADHD nervous system is, broadly speaking, one that is often simultaneously under-stimulated and over-reactive. Research published in the Journal of Attention Disorders found that ADHD adults show atypical emotional regulation characterized by quicker escalation to strong emotional responses and more difficulty returning to baseline once activated (Shaw et al., 2014). In parenting terms, this means that the ADHD parent may reach the sympathetic activation threshold faster than they expect and recover from it more slowly.

When both of these patterns are present in the same parent, the result is a nervous system that starts each day closer to threshold than a neurotypical parent's, escalates faster under stress, and takes longer to recover. Knowing this is not a reason for despair. It is information that changes what effective self-care and preparation need to look like.

Consider Dunstan (name changed), a single parent raising two children, the younger of whom has a confirmed PDA profile. Dunstan received an AuDHD diagnosis at thirty-one, several years after his younger child's. He describes the period before his diagnosis as one in which he genuinely believed he was not suited to be a parent. Every day he reached a point, usually between three and five in the afternoon, where he had nothing left. He would sit in the kitchen while his younger child escalated in the next room and feel something he could only describe as total internal silence. He was not choosing not to respond. His system had shut down. After his diagnosis, Dunstan started working with a therapist who understood polyvagal states. What he learned changed his approach entirely. The afternoon collapse was not moral failure. It was dorsal vagal shutdown triggered by cumulative sensory and emotional load without adequate recovery time during the day. The intervention was not about trying harder in the afternoon. It was about building in recovery periods earlier in the day, before the shutdown occurred.

What Interoception Has to Do With It

Interoception is the brain's ability to sense what is happening inside the body. Heart rate. Hunger. Muscle tension. The early signs of a stress response building. For many autistic people, interoceptive awareness is significantly different from the neurotypical baseline, either more intense and difficult to filter, or reduced in ways that make it hard to notice internal states until they are already acute (Garfinkel et al., 2016).

This has direct consequences for nervous system regulation. If you cannot reliably notice that your stress levels are rising until you are already in full sympathetic activation, you lose the window for early intervention. The point at which calming strategies are most effective, and the point at which they are still possible to implement, is earlier in the escalation curve, not at the peak.

Many AuDHD adults have been told, in various ways, to notice their feelings and respond to them before they become overwhelming. The difficulty is that interoceptive differences can make this genuinely hard. The emotional experience is not absent. It is either arriving in floods once it crosses a threshold, or it is present as a constant low background hum that the person has learned, through decades of adaptation, to ignore.

Building interoceptive awareness is not about trying harder to notice feelings. It is about developing body-based signals that arrive early and clearly enough to be useful. For many AuDHD adults, this requires deliberate and sustained practice.

Some practical starting points. A brief body scan at predictable times, not during a crisis but at set points in the day, can build the habit of checking in before the system overloads. Physical sensations that reliably precede emotional escalation, such as jaw tension, shallow breathing, or a change in temperature perception, can be identified over time and used as early signals. This is not comfortable work, and it does not happen quickly. But it is among the most functionally useful things an AuDHD parent can do for their own nervous system and therefore for their child.

Consider Jory (name changed), whose daughter has a PDA profile and who identifies as AuDHD without formal diagnosis. Jory had always been described as someone who went from zero to overwhelmed with no warning. She would be managing, and then she would not be, and the transition felt instantaneous to everyone, including her. Through a course of somatic therapy, she began to identify what was actually happening in the earlier stages. A specific tightening across her upper back. A change in the quality of her hearing, where sounds seemed to get sharper. A faint nausea. These physical sensations had always been there. She had not had a way to connect them to an approaching emotional state. Once she could, she had a window, small but real, to intervene before she reached the point of no return. Her intervention was simple: she would tell her daughter she needed five minutes, take those minutes in a different room with a weighted blanket, and return in a state that was at least partially recovered. The key was catching it early enough. The interoceptive work made that possible.

Building Your Own Regulation

Co-regulation, the process by which one nervous system helps another return to a more settled state, works through the ventral vagal system. A calm, regulated adult presence communicates safety to a child's nervous system through voice tone, body language, facial expression, and physical proximity. This happens largely below the level of conscious thought, through what Porges calls neuroception, the nervous system's unconscious detection of safety or threat cues in the environment (Porges, 2011).

For this to work, the adult's nervous system has to actually be in, or at least approaching, the ventral vagal zone. You cannot fake it. A parent who is visibly tense, speaking in a clipped voice, and moving with urgency is not communicating safety regardless of the words they are using.

So what does regulation look like for an AuDHD parent, practically?

Bottom-up strategies, those that work through the body rather than through thought, are generally more effective than top-down approaches for people with AuDHD. Trying to think your way to calm is less reliable than using physical input to shift the nervous system's state.

Slow, extended exhales activate the parasympathetic system and move the nervous system toward ventral vagal. The exhale does not need to be practiced in a visible or dramatic way. A slow breath out through pursed lips, done quietly in the kitchen while filling a glass of water, produces a measurable shift.

Proprioceptive input, the sensory feedback from pressure and resistance, tends to be regulating for autistic nervous systems. Pressing hands together firmly, holding a weighted blanket, or placing feet flat and pressing them into the floor are small, quick, and can be done without leaving the room.

Cold water on the wrists or face engages the dive reflex, a physiological response that slows heart rate rapidly. This is particularly useful for acute sympathetic activation.

Movement, even very brief movement, can interrupt a building stress response. Walking to another room, going up and down the stairs once, or doing ten seconds of something physically effortful creates a circuit breaker.

None of these are permanent solutions. They are tools for the moment. The longer-term work of building regulation capacity involves sleep, sensory management, consistent recovery time, and in many cases professional support. But the moment-to-moment tools matter enormously for a parent who needs to return to a usable state quickly and repeatedly throughout a day.

When to Put Yourself First

For many parents, especially those who have internalized messages about selflessness as a parenting virtue, the idea of prioritizing their own state can feel wrong. This is particularly common for parents who have also internalized shame about their neurodivergence and who approach parenting as something they need to do perfectly to compensate.

The reality is this. You cannot get on a regulated nervous system and hand it to your child if yours is offline. Trying to co-regulate from a state of full dysregulation does not produce a calmed child. It produces two dysregulated people, one small and one adult-sized, both feeding back into the other's threat response.

Prioritizing your own regulation is not abandonment. It is the functional prerequisite for being any use at all. A three-to-five minute genuine recovery period, if it returns you to a usable state, is more valuable to your child than thirty minutes of you trying to manage their distress while you are flooding.

The shame piece matters here. Many AuDHD parents carry significant shame about the moments when they cannot hold it together. Chapter 4.0 addresses that directly in the context of dual meltdowns. For now, the important point is that if you are going to build any of the skills in this book, including the ones in every chapter that follows, your nervous system needs to be in a state where skill use is possible.

Consider Larkin (name changed), a parent who described her approach to her son's PDA parenting in the following way: she had read every book. She had the strategies memorized. And when her son was in crisis, she could not access any of them. Her brain went blank. Her voice came out wrong. She said and did things she had specifically planned not to say and do. What she eventually understood, with support, was that no strategy is accessible from the sympathetic activation state. The strategies were available to the version of her that was regulated. They were not available to the version of her that was flooding. The work was not to learn more strategies. It was to get herself regulated quickly enough that the strategies she already knew became usable.

Your Next Steps

The material in this chapter builds on what the introduction established about the heritability and interaction of AuDHD and PDA. As we explored in the Introduction, recognizing the neurological basis for what is happening in your household is the first step toward working with it rather than against it.

Two things are worth taking from this chapter and sitting with before moving forward.

The first is that your state is not a luxury. It is the ground from which everything else in this book has to operate. If there is one place to invest time and effort, it is in understanding what your own nervous system needs to stay in a workable range.

The second is that bottom-up strategies, those that work through the body, are more reliable for AuDHD nervous systems than approaches that require thinking your way to calm. Identify two or three that feel possible for your particular sensory profile. Practice them in calm moments, not just crisis ones. Availability in crisis depends on how embedded they are outside of it.

The chapters ahead build on this foundation. Chapter 3.0 looks at low-demand parenting through the specific lens of what is possible for an AuDHD brain with compromised executive function. But none of that is fully accessible without the nervous system work this chapter describes.

29

Chapter 3.0 Dropping Demands When You Barely Manage Your Own

The Real Problem with Low-Demand Parenting Advice

Most low-demand parenting guidance is written for parents who have cognitive bandwidth to spare. It assumes a parent who can hold multiple things in mind at once, who remembers between interactions how they planned to respond, who can consistently frame requests indirectly even when tired, and who can maintain that approach day after day without structural support. It assumes, in other words, a neurotypical parent who has read a book and is now applying what they learned.

That description does not fit you.

Low-demand parenting is genuinely the most effective approach for children with PDA profiles. The research on this is consistent. Work on PDA in practice has established that reducing demands, sharing control, and prioritizing the child's sense of autonomy consistently produces better outcomes than behavioral or consequence-based approaches (Ross & Sparrow, 2019). That is not in question.

The question is how to apply a low-demand approach when your own executive function is compromised by ADHD, your cognitive load is already high from autistic sensory and social processing, and you are doing this in a household where the baseline level of demand is elevated by definition. That is a different problem. And it requires a different solution.

This chapter is about that solution. It starts not with what you do for your child but with what you do to your environment, because environment design is the difference between a strategy that works in theory and one that works on a Thursday afternoon when everything is already hard.

What Executive Dysfunction Actually Costs

Executive function is the set of cognitive processes that govern planning, initiating tasks, managing time, holding information in working memory, and regulating attention. In ADHD, these processes are unreliable in ways that are well documented and widely misunderstood.

The misunderstanding matters here. ADHD executive dysfunction is not laziness. It is not a failure of motivation or character. Research led by Russell Barkley has established that ADHD is fundamentally a disorder of self-regulation and response inhibition, not attention per se, and that the deficits involved are neurological in origin and inconsistent in expression (Barkley, 2012). This inconsistency is one of the most confusing features of ADHD for people who have it and for the people around them. You can do something perfectly on a Monday and completely fail to do it on a Wednesday. The task has not changed. The capacity available to you has.

For an AuDHD parent trying to implement low-demand parenting, this inconsistency creates a specific kind of trouble. Low-demand parenting is, in some ways, a high-executive-function task. It requires you to override your default communication patterns, to plan your phrasing before you open your mouth, to notice your child's state before you introduce a demand, and to adapt when something is not working. All of that requires the prefrontal cortex to be online and accessible. Under stress, or cognitive depletion, or sensory overload, it often is not.

And autistic processing adds its own cost. Many autistic people experience cognitive fatigue from the sustained effort of processing sensory information, managing social demands, and masking across the day. By the time the late afternoon arrives and the household is at its most chaotic, the AuDHD parent may have very little processing capacity left. This is when low-demand parenting is most needed and hardest to deliver.

The solution is not to try harder. The solution is to reduce the cognitive demands on yourself so that more of your available capacity is free for your child.

Consider Godric (name changed), a parent who had been told repeatedly by professionals that low-demand parenting was the answer for his daughter's PDA profile. He understood it conceptually. He had read the books. He attended the training day. And for approximately two days after each piece of input, he could apply the approach. Then life resumed its normal pace, his cognitive load climbed back to its usual level, and the strategies dissolved. He would find himself in the same interactions as before, asking his daughter to do things directly, escalating when she refused, and wondering why he could not sustain what he had understood so clearly in the calm of a training room. What Godric eventually recognized, with the support of an ADHD coach, was that the strategies required more working memory than he reliably had available. The work was not to try harder to remember them. It was to reduce the cognitive overhead of everything else so the strategies had a chance.

Simplifying Your Environment First

The principle here is that cognitive bandwidth is a limited daily resource. Everything that consumes it, from decision-making to sensory processing to managing household complexity, leaves less of it available for the demanding work of PDA-aware parenting. If you want more capacity for your child, you need to spend less of it elsewhere.

This is not a new idea. Research on decision fatigue has consistently shown that the quality of decision-making declines as the number of decisions made in a day increases, and that this effect is more pronounced in individuals with self-regulation difficulties (Hagger et al., 2010). An AuDHD parent making fifty small household decisions before noon is arriving at the afternoon's parenting challenges with a depleted resource pool.

The practical implication is environmental simplification. Not minimalism for its own sake, but deliberate reduction of the cognitive overhead of daily life. What this looks like in practice is specific. Meals on a rotation rather than planned daily reduce the decision load around food. Clothing that is already sensory-safe and laid out the night before removes one friction point from the morning. Household objects with fixed locations remove the working memory cost of tracking where things are. Predictable structure in the day, not rigid scheduling but predictable anchors, reduces the number of things requiring active planning.

The goal is not perfection. The goal is to identify the three or four specific daily tasks that consume disproportionate executive function and address those. Not all of them. Not perfectly. Just the biggest drains.

And critically: simplifying your environment is itself a demand. It takes energy and planning to implement. The way to do it for an ADHD brain is not to sit down and overhaul everything in one afternoon. It is to make one change, let it stabilize, notice whether it helps, and then make one more. Iterative, small, observable.

Consider Ivor (name changed), who identified through a week of rough tracking that the most cognitively expensive part of his day was the thirty-minute window before school. He was simultaneously managing his own sensory overload from the morning noise level, tracking multiple tasks for two children, and keeping his PDA-profiled son's demand load low enough that the day could start without a crisis. He could not reduce the fact that mornings required multiple things to happen. But he could reduce how many of those things required active thinking. He spent a weekend creating a visual anchor board for the morning sequence, not for his son but for himself. Each step was written out in the order it needed to happen. He stopped having to hold the sequence in working memory. The morning did not become easy. But his cognitive load dropped enough that he had more left over for his son's state, which was where his attention was actually needed.

Building Household Systems That Survive ADHD

A household system is any structure that reduces the number of real-time decisions required to keep things functioning. For ADHD parents, systems are not optional extras. They are the scaffolding that makes sustained low-demand parenting possible.

The difficulty is that ADHD and systems have a complicated relationship. Many ADHD adults have spent years building systems that work brilliantly for two weeks and then collapse. The collapse is not personal failure. It is a predictable feature of how ADHD interacts with routine. Novelty sustains engagement; familiarity erodes it. A system that is new and interesting will be used. A system that has become familiar and slightly effortful will be abandoned.

Research on habit formation and ADHD has found that the standard advice about building habits does not apply in the same way for ADHD brains. ADHD adults may need external cues and reward structures to maintain systems long after neurotypical people would have internalized them (Solanto, 2011). This means effective household systems for ADHD parents need to be externally visible, as simple as possible, and connected to something that provides a functional return.

Practically: systems that live inside your head do not work reliably for ADHD. Systems that are physical and visible in the environment have a much better success rate. A printed low-demand phrase list on the fridge is available when working memory is depleted. A designated physical location for every commonly lost object removes a friction point that costs cognitive load every time it comes up. A shared digital task manager, set up once and maintained minimally, removes the daily overhead of tracking what needs to happen.

The other important principle is that PDA-aware household systems need to account for the child's demand sensitivity at the design stage, not as an afterthought. A household system that requires your child to comply with a structured sequence will fail regardless of how well-organized it is. Systems that offer genuine choice within a structure, giving the child agency over timing and method rather than just outcome, are more likely to survive contact with a PDA nervous system.

And they need to be survivable when they partially collapse, because they will. ADHD inconsistency means every system will have days when it does not get followed. The question is not whether the system will occasionally fail. The question is whether a partial failure is recoverable without the whole structure dissolving. Simpler systems fail more gracefully. A morning anchor list that gets ignored on Tuesday can resume on Wednesday. A complex behavioral chart that fails once tends to be abandoned entirely.

Consider Kenrick (name changed), a parent with combined-type ADHD who had a PDA-profiled daughter and who had tried and abandoned more household systems than he could count. What finally worked for him was a single sheet of paper on the kitchen wall listing the five highest-frequency low-demand phrasings he wanted to use with his daughter. Not a full script. Not a behavioral plan. Just five phrases, written in his own handwriting, posted at eye level at the specific location in the kitchen where most morning negotiations happened. He did not need to remember the phrases. He needed to glance sideways. The system worked because it required almost nothing to maintain and delivered the specific support exactly where the need was highest. It has been on the wall for two years. He reprints it when it gets grubby.

What Good Enough Actually Means

The phrase good enough parenting comes from the psychoanalytic tradition, from Donald Winnicott's concept of the good enough mother, and it has been considerably misunderstood. Winnicott was not saying that mediocre parenting is acceptable. He was saying that perfect parenting is not only unattainable but actually counterproductive, that children need parents who fail in small ways and repair those failures, because that cycle of rupture and repair is how children develop resilience (Winnicott, 1953).

For AuDHD parents of PDA children, good enough parenting is not a lowered standard. It is a recalibration toward what is actually achievable, consistently, with the brain and the household you have. And it is genuinely what your child needs.

Your child does not need perfect low-demand parenting every moment of every day. They need a parent whose approach is good enough often enough that their nervous system experiences a net sense of safety. The hard days, the days when you default to direct demands and things escalate, do not erase the good days. They are repaired by what happens afterwards. Chapter 4.0 addresses that repair process in detail.

What good enough requires in practice is clarity about what matters most. In a PDA household, the things that matter most are the child's felt sense of safety and the parent's capacity to co-regulate. If the kitchen is messier than you would prefer, that does not matter in any functional sense. If your child's uniform is wrong on a Tuesday, that does not matter either, not if making it right would require a demand that triggers dysregulation. Good enough parenting means consistently asking which things are actually worth pressing for, and finding that the answer is almost always: fewer than you thought.

This is hard for many AuDHD parents because both autism and ADHD can produce strong responses to things being wrong or imperfect. The autistic drive toward a particular order, and the ADHD frustration when things do not go as planned, can both push against the radical acceptance that low-demand parenting ultimately requires. That push is worth noticing without necessarily acting on it. Your discomfort at something being imperfect is not always a signal that action is required. Sometimes it is just information about your own state.

Radical Acceptance as a Practical Tool

Radical acceptance is a concept developed within Dialectical Behavior Therapy. It refers to the complete acknowledgment of reality as it is, without resistance, without the added suffering that comes from fighting what cannot be changed in this moment (Linehan, 1993).

In the context of PDA parenting, radical acceptance is not passive. It is not giving up or lowering standards. It is recognizing that the demand your child is refusing is not going to happen right now, that continuing to press for it will make things worse, and then genuinely releasing the demand rather than withdrawing it with visible resentment.

The genuinely releasing part matters. PDA children are highly attuned to the social and emotional environment. A parent who has technically stopped asking for something but who is visibly tense about not getting it is still communicating a demand through their body. The child's nervous system picks this up. The demand has not gone away; it has just changed form.

Radical acceptance, practically applied, is the moment when you decide that the homework is not happening today and you actually let it go rather than letting it occupy your mental space for the rest of the evening. It is deciding that the shoes can go on in the car. It is deciding that dinner does not require sitting at the table if sitting at the table is the thing standing between you and a manageable evening.

For an AuDHD parent, radical acceptance is also useful as a self-directed practice. Many AuDHD parents carry a running internal critique of their own parenting performance that adds to their cognitive load and depletes their available capacity. The difficult morning, the escalation you handled badly, the system that collapsed: these are real events. They do not require continued mental processing once the moment has passed. Radical acceptance of your own imperfect performance is one of the most useful cognitive load reduction strategies available.

The Environment Over Willpower Principle

Everything in this chapter comes back to one underlying principle. Environment design is more reliable than willpower for the AuDHD parent.

Willpower, understood as the determined application of cognitive effort to override default behavior, is a depleting resource that performs worst when you need it most. At three in the afternoon, after a day of sensory overload and executive demands, the willpower-based approach to low-demand parenting fails. Not because you do not care enough. Because the resource has been used up.

Environment design does not deplete. A phrase list on the wall is available at three in the afternoon in exactly the same way it was available at nine in the morning. A simplified morning routine that removed four daily decisions saves cognitive load every morning regardless of what kind of night preceded it. A household structure that reduced inadvertent demands on your child does not require you to remember to implement it.

The investment is up front. The return is ongoing. And the cumulative effect of many small environmental changes is a household in which low-demand parenting is easier to do because the environment has been shaped to support it.

This does not mean the environment can do the parenting. There are moments in every PDA household that require your full presence and your best regulated response. The goal of environment design is to make sure you arrive at those moments with more capacity than you would have had otherwise.

Essential Points

Low-demand parenting is the right approach for PDA children. The challenge for AuDHD parents is applying it consistently with an executive function profile that makes consistency difficult.

The answer is not to try harder. It is to reduce the cognitive overhead of the household environment so more capacity is available for the work of PDA-aware parenting.

Effective household systems for ADHD parents are externally visible, as simple as possible, designed to survive partial failure, and built for the real household rather than an ideal one.

Good enough parenting is not a compromised standard. It is a calibration toward what is consistently achievable. The rupture and repair cycle is as important as the high-functioning moments, and it is the subject of the next chapter.

Radical acceptance of both the child's demand avoidance and your own parenting imperfections is a practical cognitive load reduction strategy. Build the environment to support the right responses. Do not rely on willpower alone to produce them.

Chapter 4.0 Meltdowns Times 2 When Your Child's Crisis Triggers Yours

What the Cascade Actually Looks Like

Most accounts of parenting through a child's meltdown describe it from the outside. The adult contains the crisis. The adult provides a steady presence. The adult waits it out without escalating.

This is accurate, as far as it goes. What it does not describe is what happens inside the parent's body during that process in a double neurodivergent household. It does not describe the auditory sensitivity that makes the volume of a meltdown physically painful. It does not describe the fight-or-flight activation that arrives uninvited when a child's distress signal enters the room. It does not describe the working memory collapse that happens under stress, where the scripts you planned and the strategies you know simply are not accessible. It does not describe the shame that arrives in the aftermath, when the crisis is over and you are left with the memory of your own voice, raised, and your own hands, too tight, and the knowledge that you are a person who researched PDA and still made it worse.

The cascade is the sequence that begins when your child's crisis triggers your own dysregulation, and your dysregulation amplifies your child's crisis, which amplifies yours, and so on until someone exits the interaction or something breaks the cycle by force.

Understanding the cascade is the first step toward interrupting it. And interrupting it, even partially, even late, is always worth doing.

The Neuroscience of the Cascade

When a PDA child reaches the point of meltdown, their nervous system has moved into full sympathetic activation or dorsal vagal shutdown. The behaviors that result, including screaming, physical aggression, flight, or complete withdrawal, are not chosen or controllable by the child in that state. They are the output of a nervous system that has registered overwhelming threat and is responding accordingly.

For the AuDHD parent in the same space, the child's distress signal is processed through a nervous system that already operates closer to its activation threshold. Research on threat contagion has found that emotional distress signals, particularly those involving sound and facial expression, activate mirror neuron systems and autonomic threat responses in observers, with higher sensitivity in individuals with atypical sensory and social processing profiles (Iacoboni, 2009). The autistic parent, who may process emotional signals from others with particular intensity, and the ADHD parent, who has reduced capacity to inhibit reactive responses, are both more likely than a neurotypical parent to have their own nervous system activated by their child's crisis.

When the parent's nervous system activates, their voice changes. Their body posture changes. Their facial expression changes. The PDA child's threat-detection system, which is already hyper-alert, picks up all of these signals and reads them as additional threat. The child's dysregulation intensifies. Which intensifies the parent's response. This is the cascade. It is mutual, it is rapid, and it is not the fault of either person.

Knowing this does not automatically stop the cascade from happening. But it provides the interpretive frame that makes recovery possible: neither you nor your child was choosing to make it worse. You were both doing what your nervous systems do.

Building a Safety Plan for Dual Dysregulation

A safety plan for dual dysregulation is not a crisis management procedure in the clinical sense. It is a pre-decided set of steps that you know, before anything goes wrong, you will use when a cascade begins. Its purpose is to make good decisions available at the moment when your capacity to make good decisions is lowest.

The plan has four components.

The first is a physical signal that tells you the cascade has begun. Not a thought, because thoughts become unreliable under activation. A physical signal: a specific feeling in your body, a specific behavior in your child, or a specific point in the interaction that you have identified in advance as the threshold. Crispin, who appeared in Chapter 1.0, identified his signal as the moment when his hearing sharpened. Jory, from Chapter 2.0, identified it as a tightening across her upper back. Your signal will be specific to you. The work is to identify it now, when you are calm, rather than trying to identify it in the middle of a crisis.

The second component is a scripted exit from the interaction. Not an abandonment. A brief, neutral statement that communicates you are stepping back without communicating anger or rejection. Something like: "I am going to the kitchen for a few minutes." Or: "I need some space for a moment." The exact words matter less than the fact that they are pre-decided, short, and said in the calmest tone you can manage at that point. Pre-deciding them means you do not have to generate language under stress. You have it ready.

The third component is a specific regulation tool you will use in that window. Not a list of options. One thing. The one thing that most reliably moves your nervous system toward a more settled state. For some people this is cold water on the face. For some it is a brief period of physical pressure. For some it is a specific sensory item. The regularity of the tool matters more than the sophistication of it. The tool you use ten times a month is more effective than the optimal tool you use twice.

The fourth component is a re-entry. A decision about how you will return to your child after the window. What you will say first. How you will signal that the interaction can restart without pressure. This is the moment when repair begins, and having a pre-decided re-entry phrase removes the cognitive overhead of finding the right words while still partially activated.

Consider Merrick (name changed), who has an AuDHD diagnosis and whose twelve-year-old son has a confirmed PDA profile. Merrick had spent two years in what he described as a weekly cycle of escalation and recovery. The escalations were predictable in retrospect, always following the same sequence of trigger, avoidance, demand, resistance, and eventual meltdown from both of them, but in the moment they felt uncontrollable. The safety plan he developed with a PDA-specialist family therapist was exactly four steps: notice the jaw tension that always preceded his own activation; say "I'm stepping out for a bit" without additional content; do thirty seconds of pressing his palms against the wall in the hallway; return and say "I'm back, no agenda." The plan did not stop every cascade. But it shortened them significantly. And each time he implemented it, even partially, it disrupted the sequence enough that his son's nervous system had a chance to begin settling.

When the Plan Does Not Work

There will be times when the cascade happens before you reach the signal. There will be times when you implement the exit and your child's distress escalates further because they experience your withdrawal as abandonment. There will be times when the regulation window is too short and you return still activated. There will be times when you say something you planned not to say and do something you planned not to do.

These are not failures of the plan. They are the expected output of two dysregulated nervous systems in a high-stakes interaction. The plan is not designed to produce perfection. It is designed to produce a more recoverable situation than you would have had without it.

What matters after the plan does not work is not the fact that it did not work. It is what you do next. And what you do next is the repair conversation.

The Repair Conversation

Repair is not an apology. Or rather, an apology is not sufficient for repair, and in some circumstances, an apology is not the right starting point at all.

Research on repair conversations in attachment theory has established that ruptures in the parent-child relationship are universal and that their effect on the child's development depends almost entirely on whether repair follows (Siegel & Hartzell, 2003). Children who experience consistent rupture and repair develop the understanding that relationships can withstand difficulty and recover. Children who experience rupture without repair develop a different understanding entirely.

For PDA children specifically, repair conversations require care. A direct, confrontational approach to repair, even a well-intentioned one, can itself feel like a demand. Sitting the child down and asking them to discuss what happened is a demand. Requiring them to engage with their feelings about the incident is a demand. Pressing for eye contact, verbal response, or any specific form of engagement is a demand.

Effective repair with a PDA child tends to be indirect. It might look like sitting near them without initiating conversation, and eventually saying something low-key and observation-based: "That was a hard one." It might look like a note left somewhere they will find it. It might look like offering something they enjoy without any connection to the earlier crisis. It might look like returning to normal activity as if the rupture is no longer the organizing event of the relationship, because it is not.

The repair is complete not when the child has acknowledged what happened or expressed forgiveness, but when the relationship has returned to a felt sense of safety on both sides.

Repair with yourself is a different and equally important process. Many AuDHD parents carry the aftermath of cascade incidents for hours or days, replaying what happened and generating shame about their own behavior. This internal processing has a cost. It continues to consume cognitive and emotional resources, it colors subsequent interactions with the child, and it can produce a hypervigilant parenting state that is itself a source of demand on the child's nervous system.

The repair conversation you have with yourself after a cascade follows a similar structure to the one with your child. Acknowledgment without catastrophizing. Recognition of what happened without prolonged self-punishment. And then, genuinely, letting it go.

Consider Oswin (name changed), whose daughter has a PDA profile and who describes her own emotional response profile as one where activation arrives quickly and shame arrives immediately after. Her repair conversations with her daughter had consistently failed because she kept opening them with apologies that required a response. "I'm so sorry I shouted" produced in her daughter either a flat silence or a fresh wave of upset, because it was still a demand, still an invitation to process the incident, still a way of re-entering the event rather than leaving it behind. What eventually worked was something much smaller. She would wait until her daughter had begun to regulate, then come into the same room and start doing something ordinary, folding laundry, making a snack, without directing any attention toward her daughter. If her daughter came near, she would say something brief and neutral. If her daughter did not come near, she said nothing at all. The repair happened through proximity and the absence of further demand. Her daughter, over time, began to initiate contact after these periods. Not to discuss the incident. Simply to re-establish connection. That was the repair.

Repair Scripts You Can Actually Use

For PDA children, repair scripts need to be short, low-demand, and free of anything that requires the child to perform a particular emotional response.

Some options that work across different ages and contexts:

"That was rough. I'm glad we're both still here." "I got it wrong in there. You don't need to say anything about it." "I'm not still upset. We can just move on whenever you're ready." "I'm going to make some hot chocolate. You can have some if you want."

These are not magic phrases. Their effectiveness depends on the relationship context and the child's current state. But they share a structure: they acknowledge the rupture briefly, they release the child from any obligation to respond, and they signal that the parent's nervous system has returned to a baseline.

For yourself, when the cascade is over and you are in the aftermath:

"That happened. I did not handle it the way I wanted to. I can make a repair and then move forward." "I know more than I was able to use in that moment. That is how activation works, not how much I care about my child." "The hard moment is over. What happens next is what matters."

These are not about bypassing the difficulty of what happened. They are about not extending it beyond its natural duration.

Self-Compassion as a Functional Strategy

The shame that follows a cascade is not incidental. It is one of the most functionally damaging parts of the whole sequence, and it is worth addressing directly because it gets in the way of effective parenting.

Shame differs from guilt in a specific way that matters here. Guilt says: I did something wrong and I can do something about it. Shame says: I am wrong, and there is nothing to do about it. Guilt is a productive state that can motivate repair and behavior change. Shame is not. Shame produces withdrawal, self-protection, and avoidance of the very relationship repair that the situation requires (Brown, 2010).

For AuDHD parents who already carry substantial histories of being told they are too much, too intense, too inconsistent, too emotional: the shame after a parenting cascade lands in a prepared bed. It confirms a story about yourself that was already running. That is why it is so potent and why it can persist long after the practical situation has been resolved.

Self-compassion, in the specific sense described by Kristin Neff's research, is not self-indulgence. It is the recognition that suffering is part of the shared human experience, that treating yourself with the same kindness you would extend to another person in the same situation is not weak but necessary, and that harsh self-judgment does not produce better outcomes; it produces more dysregulation (Neff, 2011).

In practical terms for the AuDHD parent: the question to ask after a cascade is not "what is wrong with me that I responded that way?" The question is "what would I say to another AuDHD parent who had just been through exactly this, and how do I say that to myself?"

You would not tell that parent they should have known better. You would not tell them their neurodivergence is an excuse. You would not tell them that their child is going to be damaged by the fact that this happened. You would tell them that this is hard, that they are doing something genuinely difficult, that repair is possible, and that showing up again is what counts. That is what you say to yourself.

Consider Quinlan (name changed), an AuDHD parent who worked in a caring profession and who described a particular contradiction at the centre of her parenting: she was very good at offering compassion to the families she worked with and entirely unable to apply the same quality of response to herself. After a cascade incident with her PDA-profiled son, she would spend the rest of the day in a state she described as low-grade internal prosecution, replaying what had happened and generating increasingly harsh verdicts. She recognized this as neither useful nor kind when a colleague described doing the same thing, but she could not stop it by knowing it was counterproductive. What eventually helped was a specific and deliberate practice: she wrote out what she would say to a parent who had described her exact cascade to her in a professional context. She wrote it fully, in the professional voice she used at work. Then she read what she had written. The gap between the care she offered others and the judgment she applied to herself was, when made visible, impossible to ignore. She began using the written exercise after cascade incidents, not to generate the same compassion immediately, but to close the gap gradually. Over several months, the internal prosecution shortened. It did not disappear. But it no longer ran for the rest of the day.

What Both of You Need Afterwards

After a cascade has resolved and some degree of repair has happened, both you and your child need recovery time. This is not a luxury and it is not negotiable. The nervous system does not return to baseline instantaneously, and continuing to demand high-functioning engagement from either party immediately after a crisis produces a second smaller cascade.

For the child: low demand, low sensory input, access to their preferred regulatory activities, and no processing of the incident unless they initiate it.

For the parent: the same principle applies. A brief period of legitimate recovery, whatever form that takes for your particular sensory and emotional profile, is not self-indulgence. It is the preparation for the next interaction.

And then: you continue. Not because the hard moment did not happen. Because it did, and repair happened, and the relationship is intact. That continuation, that returning to ordinary life after something difficult, is itself one of the most important things a parent can communicate to a child. The relationship survived. It is safe to come back.

Essential Points

The cascade effect in the double-ND household is the sequence by which a child's meltdown triggers the parent's dysregulation, which amplifies the child's distress, which amplifies the parent's response. It is mutual, neurologically driven, and not the fault of either person.

A safety plan for dual dysregulation has four components: a physical early-warning signal, a pre-scripted exit from the interaction, a single specific regulation tool, and a pre-decided re-entry phrase.

Repair with a PDA child needs to be indirect, low-demand, and free of any requirement for the child to perform a specific emotional response. Repair with yourself requires acknowledgment without catastrophizing and release without prolonged self-punishment.

Shame after a cascade is one of the most functionally damaging parts of the sequence. Self-compassion is not weakness. It is the practical precondition for effective repair and continued regulated parenting.

Both you and your child need recovery time after a cascade. That recovery is the preparation for showing up again. And showing up again is the job.

Chapter 5.0 Communication Between Two Different Neurodivergent Brains

The Communication Problem No One Names

There is a specific communication mismatch at the centre of the double-ND household that no standard PDA parenting guide fully addresses. It is the one that happens when autistic directness meets PDA avoidance. When the ADHD brain that has been holding a request for the last forty minutes finally runs out of patience and just says the thing. When the most efficient route between a parent's intention and a child's action turns out to be the one that guarantees escalation.

Most guidance on communicating with PDA children correctly identifies that demands need to be framed indirectly, that declarative language is more effective than instructional language, and that reducing the demand load in everyday speech significantly reduces the frequency of avoidance responses. All of that is accurate.

What it does not address is the particular difficulty of applying those principles when you are autistic, which means your natural communication style runs toward directness and efficiency, and when you have ADHD, which means your impulse to just say the thing arrives with significant force and without much warning.

This chapter is about that specific problem. It does not ask you to become a different kind of communicator. It offers tools that can work within the communication profile you actually have, including the parts that make PDA parenting advice difficult to follow in the moment.

What Autistic Directness Actually Is

Autistic communication tends to be direct, literal, and efficient. When an autistic person has information to convey or a request to make, the natural form is the most direct available route: say what you mean, mean what you say, and expect the same in return. This is not rudeness or a lack of social awareness, though it has frequently been misidentified as both. It is a communication style shaped by a brain that processes language literally and finds indirection effortful and often ambiguous.

Research on autistic communication has found that autistic people consistently rate direct communication as more comfortable and less cognitively demanding than indirect or heavily implied communication (Mitchell et al., 2021). What neurotypical social conventions describe as polite indirection, autistic people often experience as vague, confusing, or potentially deceptive. The preference for directness is not a failure of social development. It is a coherent feature of the communication style.

In the context of PDA parenting, however, autistic directness creates a structural conflict. PDA children are neurologically wired to experience direct demands as threats to autonomy and safety. A clear, direct instruction, however kindly intended, is exactly the kind of communication that activates a PDA child's avoidance response most reliably. The more direct the instruction, the more explicit the demand, and the more explicit the demand, the stronger the avoidance.

This is not about tone. It is structural. An autistic parent can deliver a direct demand in the warmest possible tone and it will still land as a demand. What needs to change is not how the instruction sounds but how the instruction is formed.

What ADHD Impulsivity Does to Communication

ADHD adds another layer. The ADHD brain generates responses quickly, speaks before full processing has occurred, and has reduced capacity to inhibit verbal impulses under pressure. When the household is running late and a child has not put their shoes on, the ADHD parent's brain does not naturally generate an indirect, autonomy-preserving alternative. It generates the shortest available path to compliance: "Put your shoes on. Now."

Research on verbal impulsivity in ADHD has found that adults with ADHD demonstrate measurably higher rates of blurt behavior, speaking before planning, and difficulty modifying verbal output once initiated, compared to neurotypical adults, and that these patterns intensify under stress and time pressure (Barkley, 2015). In the specific conditions of a PDA household, where time pressure and stress are common features of many ordinary interactions, ADHD verbal impulsivity is going to produce exactly the communication that causes the most escalation at the moments when escalation is most costly.

The standard advice, to pause and think before speaking, is not wrong. But it requires the kind of executive function that is least available under the conditions when it is most needed. A better approach involves reducing the work required to generate indirect communication in the moment, which means having low-demand alternatives already loaded and accessible before the interaction begins.

This is why the phrase list on the wall, described in Chapter 3.0, is not just a household system. It is a communication tool. The ADHD brain that cannot generate an indirect alternative in the moment can glance at a physical resource and find one ready.

Declarative Language: What It Is and Why It Works

Declarative language is speech that makes observations, describes states, and shares thinking, without directing or instructing. It is the opposite of imperative language, which is speech that tells someone what to do.

Imperative language: "Put your shoes on." Declarative language: "I notice your shoes are still by the door."

Imperative language: "Come for dinner." Declarative language: "Dinner is ready. I'm going to sit down."

Imperative language: "Stop doing that." Declarative language: "I'm finding that sound quite difficult to listen to."

The reason declarative language works with PDA children is that it does not create an explicit demand. It shares information. The information may imply a response, but the child's nervous system is not triggered by the implication in the same way it is triggered by the direct instruction. The child retains the felt sense of having chosen to respond, even when the response is the one the parent needed.

Research on declarative language as an intervention strategy has found that consistent use of declarative over imperative communication significantly reduced demand-avoidance responses in children with PDA profiles, while also improving the quality of spontaneous social engagement (Freed, 2019). The mechanism is understood to be the preservation of autonomy felt sense: the child is not responding to a command, they are responding to information, and the distinction matters to their nervous system even when the behavioral outcome is the same.

For the autistic parent, declarative language can feel unnatural at first. It is indirect. It requires rephrasing what you want to say into an observation about a state rather than an instruction about an action. For a communication style built on efficiency and directness, this is genuinely effortful. It can also feel dishonest, like wrapping a demand in a disguise instead of just saying what you mean.

This feeling is worth addressing directly. Declarative language is not dishonest. You are not hiding a demand. You are sharing accurate information in a way that does not activate your child's threat response. The statement "dinner is ready, I'm going to sit down" is entirely true. The fact that it also functions as an indirect invitation to join you does not make it deceptive. It makes it adapted communication, the same kind of adaptation that humans make constantly in social contexts.

Scripts for Under-Stress Conditions

The difficulty with communication scripts is that they need to be retrievable at exactly the moments when retrieval is hardest: under stress, when working memory is depleted, when the ADHD verbal impulse has already formed the direct version and is waiting to be spoken.

The scripts that work in these conditions have a few shared features. They are short. They are true. They require minimal modification for different situations. And they have been practiced enough in low-stakes conditions that they have some automaticity when high-stakes conditions arrive.

Here is a practical set organized by common high-frequency demand situations.

For transitions: "I'm heading upstairs in about five minutes." "The food's nearly ready." "It's starting to get toward bedtime."

For activities that need to stop: "I'm starting to feel like I need the noise to come down a bit." "This space is going to need clearing before we can do the next thing." "I notice it's been a while since anyone moved around."

For hygiene and self-care: "The shower is free whenever." "I put a clean towel in there." "There's a toothbrush ready."

For food and mealtimes: "I made enough for everyone." "I'm going to eat now, while it's warm." "There's food in the kitchen."

For leaving the house: "I'm putting my shoes on." "I've got the bag by the door." "The car is ready when you are."

These are not magic phrases. They will not work every time, and there will be days when even the most carefully formed declarative statement triggers avoidance because the child's threat level is already high for unrelated reasons. The goal is to remove the unnecessary demand load from ordinary communication, so that the avoidance that does occur is responding to something real rather than to the form of the request.

Consider Aldwyn (name changed), who was introduced in the Introduction as a parent navigating dual diagnoses with his son. His specific challenge was morning transitions, where his ADHD impulsivity produced a sequence of increasingly direct instructions that his son's PDA profile met with increasing resistance. The breakthrough for Aldwyn was not a script, exactly. It was a realization that he needed to start communicating about the transition fifteen minutes earlier, and to do it entirely in declarative form, so that by the time the transition needed to happen, his son had been processing it for long enough that it did not arrive as a sudden demand. "I'm going to start getting ready soon" planted a seed. "I'm going to the bathroom" was a neutral update. "I've got my keys" was information. By the time Aldwyn moved to the door, his son had been watching the transition approach for fifteen minutes and often initiated his own preparation without being asked. Not always. But more often than before.

Reducing Inadvertent Demands

Beyond the obvious instructional demands, there is a category of inadvertent demands that are worth identifying because they accumulate throughout the day and raise the overall demand load on the child without the parent recognizing they are doing it.

Inadvertent demands include: questions that require a verbal response ("How was your day?" "What do you want for dinner?" "Are you feeling okay?"), requests for emotional information ("Why are you upset?" "What's wrong?"), demands for attention or eye contact through body language or expectant pauses, and commentary on the child's behavior that implies a required change ("You haven't eaten much." "You're still on that screen.").

These are not malicious. They are ordinary human communication. Most children, most of the time, respond to them without difficulty. PDA children process them as demands, and the cumulative effect of a day full of small demands is a raised baseline threat level that makes the actual necessary demands, shoes, mealtimes, sleep, much harder to navigate.

Reducing inadvertent demands is a different task from learning declarative scripts. It requires noticing the patterns in your own communication: how many questions you ask, how often you comment on what the child is doing, how frequently your presence implies an expectation of response. For an ADHD brain that tends to think out loud, this can mean catching a significant number of verbal impulses before they leave the room.

One practical approach is the tracking exercise. For a single day, note every time you direct speech toward your child and loosely categorize it as either a demand or a non-demand. Most people are surprised by how much of their ordinary communication functions as a demand. The goal after the tracking exercise is not to stop communicating. It is to identify two or three specific inadvertent demand types that are high-frequency in your household and develop alternatives for those specific ones. Not everything at once. The two or three that are costing the most.

Consider Elowen (name changed), introduced in the Introduction, who recognized during a week of rough self-monitoring that she asked her daughter questions constantly. Not large questions. Small ones: "Did you sleep okay?" "Do you want a snack?" "Are you cold?" She had not thought of these as demands. They were care expressed through inquiry. But her daughter experienced them as a series of required responses, each one small, but collectively producing a demand load that accounted for a significant portion of her daily avoidance. Elowen began shifting from questions to observations: "I noticed you were up quite late" instead of "Did you sleep okay?"; "I made a snack" instead of "Do you want a snack?" The questions did not disappear entirely. But replacing the highest-frequency ones reduced the overall demand load in a way that had visible effects within a few weeks.

Adapting Communication for Your Own State

The scripts and strategies in this chapter are easier to implement on some days than others. And the days when they are hardest to implement are often the same days when implementing them matters most.

Your own cognitive and sensory state directly affects your ability to generate indirect communication. When you are depleted, dysregulated, or in sensory overload, your communication regresses toward the most automatic available form, which for most adults is direct imperative speech. This is not a failure. It is how the brain conserves resources under load.

What helps is a simple escalation awareness. When you notice you are in a higher-depletion state, before you begin an interaction that is likely to require low-demand communication, you can use that awareness as a prompt to access your prepared resources. Glance at the phrase list. Slow your pace slightly before entering the room. Take one slow exhale. These are not transformative interventions. They are small friction reducers that slightly improve the chances of generating an indirect alternative over a direct demand.

There is also a version of self-disclosure that works in some PDA households, particularly as children get older. When a parent can say genuinely and without distress, "I'm having a hard sensory day, so my words might come out wrong, I'm going to try to say things in an easier way," this communicates both transparency about the parent's state and intention to adapt. It removes the child's need to interpret the parent's tone as a demand signal. And it models the kind of self-knowledge and self-disclosure that is a significant protective factor for neurodivergent children developing their own understanding of their needs.

This version of self-disclosure requires a level of self-awareness and regulation that is not always available. It is a useful tool for the medium-depletion days, the ones where you know it is going to be harder but you have enough to work with. It is not a tool for the days when you are fully dysregulated. On those days, the safety plan from Chapter 4.0 is the right first step.

Consider Fenwick (name changed), who appeared in Chapter 1.0 and whose ADHD-driven communication defaults had contributed to a pattern of escalation with his PDA-profiled son. After several months of working on declarative communication, he identified a specific pattern: his successes clustered on days when he had adequate sleep and time to prepare, and his failures clustered on days when he was already cognitively depleted before the first difficult interaction. He began treating his own state as the first relevant variable each morning. On the harder days, he would put the phrase list at eye level before his son was awake, so that when the first demand situation arose, the alternatives were visible before the impulse to speak directly had already formed. He also shortened his interactions on high-depletion days, reducing the total number of communication exchanges rather than trying to maintain the same interaction quality he managed on better days. Less communication, but better-formed communication, turned out to be more effective than more communication with degraded quality.

What Comes Next

The communication tools in this chapter work best when combined with the nervous system regulation practices from Chapter 2.0 and the environmental design principles from Chapter 3.0. Communication quality is downstream of regulation. A parent who has prepared their environment, managed their sensory load, and arrived at the interaction in a relatively settled state will use declarative language more naturally than a parent who is arriving depleted.

Chapter 6.0 takes these communication principles into the context of institutional advocacy, where the demands are different in kind, coming from school professionals and bureaucratic systems rather than from daily household life, but where the same underlying dynamics apply: the AuDHD parent's communication under pressure, the risk of dysregulation in high-stakes environments, and the need for pre-prepared resources that reduce the real-time cognitive demand of advocacy.

Essential Points

The communication challenge in the double-ND household is the structural mismatch between autistic directness, which tends toward clear instruction, and PDA neurology, which reads clear instruction as demand and responds with avoidance.

ADHD verbal impulsivity amplifies this mismatch. The ADHD brain under stress generates the most direct available communication. Reducing the cognitive work required to access indirect alternatives in the moment, through physical phrase lists and pre-loaded scripts, is more reliable than relying on in-the-moment generation.

Declarative language preserves the child's felt sense of autonomy by sharing information rather than issuing instructions. It is not deception. It is adapted communication that accounts for the child's neurological profile.

Inadvertent demands accumulate across the day. Identifying and reducing the highest-frequency inadvertent demand types lowers the baseline threat level and makes the necessary demands more navigable.

Your own cognitive and sensory state is the first variable in any communication interaction. Knowing your state and having resources accessible before the interaction begins improves outcomes more reliably than trying to adapt in the moment.

Chapter 6.0 School Advocacy When Institutions Trigger You Too

The Meeting You Were Not Built For

There is a particular kind of room that most AuDHD adults recognize immediately. The conference room at a school. The table with the professionals arrayed on one side. The agenda that was not circulated in advance. The fluorescent lighting and the ambient sound of institutional buildings. The sense, walking in, that you are the least qualified person in the space, even if you know more about your child than everyone else in it combined.

School advocacy is the process of representing your child's needs within educational systems that were not designed for neurodivergent children and are largely staffed by people who have received limited training in PDA specifically. It requires you to articulate complex neurological needs in terms that bureaucratic systems can process. It requires you to hold your ground when professionals who do not know your child push back on what you know to be true. It requires you to sit in rooms that are often sensory challenging, in conversations that are often emotionally charged, and to communicate with precision and persuasiveness while simultaneously managing your own threat response.

For neurotypical parents, this is hard. For AuDHD parents, it can be activating in every direction at once.

This chapter addresses school advocacy specifically through the lens of the AuDHD parent. It does not assume unlimited executive function, sensory tolerance, or emotional regulation. It offers structures that make advocacy possible with the brain you have, in rooms that are often difficult, on behalf of a child whose needs the system may be actively resisting.

How Institutions Trigger the AuDHD Parent

Understanding why school meetings are disproportionately activating for AuDHD parents is the first step toward preparing for them effectively.

The demand load in a school meeting is high and largely non-negotiable. You are required to attend at a specific time. You are required to engage with a structured agenda. You are required to produce verbal responses in real time to information that may be new or distressing. You are required to advocate while seated, often in an uncomfortable sensory environment, across from people who hold institutional authority over your child. The autonomy that AuDHD nervous systems typically require to function at their best is almost entirely absent.

For autistic adults, the social processing demands of formal institutional meetings carry a significant cognitive load. Research on autistic adults in formal professional contexts has found that the combined demands of processing social dynamics, managing presentation of self, interpreting implicit communication, and producing fluent verbal responses consistently produces faster and more complete cognitive depletion than the same content delivered in a lower-demand format (Raymaker et al., 2020). By the time a school meeting has been running for forty minutes, many autistic adults are operating in a significantly depleted state relative to where they started.

For adults with ADHD, meetings present a different but equally significant challenge. The sustained attention and executive function required to track a complex discussion, hold relevant information in working memory, and intervene at exactly the right moments are all functions that ADHD impairs. ADHD adults in meetings commonly report losing track of the discussion, missing the moment to contribute a key point, or finding the relevant thing to say only after the topic has moved on (Brown, 2013).

Rejection Sensitive Dysphoria, often abbreviated as RSD, adds a further layer. RSD is an intense emotional response to perceived rejection, criticism, or failure that is strongly associated with ADHD and produces a sudden, overwhelming affective response (Dodson, 2016). In school meetings, where professionals may dispute your child's diagnosis, minimize reported difficulties, or imply that the parenting approach is contributing to the problem, RSD can be activated acutely. The emotional response is physiologically real. It is not an overreaction. And it can significantly impair the advocacy you came to do if it arrives unexpectedly.

Preparation as the Primary Strategy

Because school meetings activate multiple AuDHD-specific difficulty areas simultaneously, preparation is the single most effective intervention available. Not preparation as a general principle, but specific, structural preparation that reduces the real-time cognitive demands of the meeting to the absolute minimum.

The goal of preparation is to answer as many questions as possible before you walk into the room, so that the in-meeting demands are limited to confirming, clarifying, and holding ground rather than generating, processing, and formulating.

Before any school meeting, five preparation steps serve AuDHD parents well.

First: obtain and review the agenda before the meeting whenever possible. If the school does not routinely circulate agendas in advance, request one explicitly. A written agenda reduces the working memory demands of tracking the meeting and allows you to prepare specific responses to predictable topics in advance.

Second: write down, in bullet points, the three to five things you most need the meeting to achieve. Not everything. The three to five most important outcomes. Having these written means that when the meeting is running long and your processing is depleted, you can glance at your notes and remember what you came for.

Third: prepare at least one response for each item on the agenda that is likely to be contested. If the school typically pushes back on a specific accommodation, prepare the sentence you will use to hold your ground. Write it down. Practice saying it once or twice, not to rehearse a performance but to reduce the retrieval effort when you need it under pressure.

Fourth: decide in advance what you will not agree to in the meeting. Any agreement to remove an accommodation, change a placement, or reduce support level should not be agreed to in the meeting itself. A phrase like "I need to take that home and think about it before I can agree to a change" is a legitimate and useful tool. Prepare it in advance so that it is available when time pressure in the meeting makes an in-the-moment decision feel necessary.

Fifth: prepare your sensory environment as well as your verbal content. This means identifying what you will need in the meeting room to maintain a functional state. Water. A fidget tool in your pocket. Permission to take notes on paper or a device rather than relying on working memory alone. If the standard meeting room is sensory-challenging, you are entitled to request a different space. That request is easier to make before the meeting than during it.

Consider Dunstan (name changed), a single parent introduced in Chapter 2.0, who had spent three years dreading his younger child's school meetings because they reliably ended with him agreeing to things he later regretted and failing to raise things he had planned to raise. His preparation practice, once established, took approximately forty-five minutes before each meeting and involved: reading any circulated documents twice, once for content and once specifically for anything that would require him to advocate or push back; writing his three key outcomes on a card; writing two sentences he might need to use if contested; and putting a stim object in his jacket pocket. The meetings did not become comfortable. But his outcomes improved significantly, and the post-meeting regret over things unsaid or unwillingly agreed to largely disappeared.

Advocacy Scripts for Common Contested Situations

PDA-specific needs are frequently contested in school settings, partly because PDA as an educational framework is not universally understood, and partly because the adaptations PDA children need run counter to many standard school approaches. The following scripts address the most common points of resistance. They are short, factual, and designed to be usable when processing is under pressure.

When a professional says the behavior is a choice: "My child's avoidance responses are neurologically driven by anxiety, not by deliberate defiance. The research on PDA profiles documents this consistently. The interventions that help are those that reduce demand load, not those that increase consequences."

When a professional says the child is doing fine at school but not at home: "School compliance in PDA profiles is often a result of masking, which is a high-cost coping strategy. The distress is deferred and presents at home. This is documented in the research on autistic masking. The absence of visible difficulty at school does not indicate absence of difficulty."

When a professional suggests the parenting approach is the problem: "The low-demand approach we use at home is evidence-based for PDA profiles and recommended by specialists who work with this neurotype. I would be happy to share the specific resources we are working from."

When a professional suggests a reward system would help: "Reward-based systems increase the demand load on PDA children because they add conditions to accessing things the child values. For our child, this consistently produces escalation rather than improved compliance. We have documented this over several months."

When being asked to agree to a change in support: "I need to take that home and review it before I can agree to a change. I will respond in writing within [timeframe]."

These scripts are not confrontational. They are factual and they hold ground without aggression. Practicing them before the meeting means they are retrievable under pressure.

When to Bring a Neurotypical Ally

There are school meeting contexts where bringing a neurotypical ally, a trusted friend, partner, or parent advocate who does not carry the same activation profile as you do, is the most pragmatic decision available.

This is not a failure of self-advocacy. It is an accurate assessment of the conditions and an appropriate use of available resources.

A neurotypical ally can monitor the meeting dynamics while you process content, can intervene if you are being steamrolled, can remember things that you missed while managing your own state, and can provide a verbal buffer in moments when your RSD is activated enough to affect the quality of your responses.

If you bring an ally, prepare them specifically. They need to know your three key outcomes. They need to know which accommodations cannot be negotiated away. They need to know that if you say a specific phrase, for example "I need a moment," they should step in. And they need to know not to over-advocate in ways that suggest you cannot speak for yourself, because you can. The ally is a resource, not a replacement.

There are also professional parent advocates and SEND caseworkers in many regions who specifically support neurodivergent families through education systems. If your child's situation is complex or contested, accessing professional advocacy support is a practical and legitimate choice, not a concession.

Consider Larkin (name changed), who appeared in Chapter 4.0 and who had avoided school meetings for a year after an incident in which her RSD was activated so acutely by a school professional's dismissiveness that she had left the meeting in tears and been unable to return. She began bringing a close friend to subsequent meetings, briefed in advance with her outcomes list. Her friend's presence did not change the school's position initially. But it changed Larkin's experience of the meeting. She was no longer alone in the room with the institutional dynamic. She had someone on her side who could witness what was happening. Her ability to advocate effectively improved substantially, not because her friend did the advocacy, but because the felt safety of not being alone activated her ventral vagal system enough that she could access her own capacity.

Managing the Meeting Environment

AuDHD parents are entitled to request reasonable adjustments to meeting environments, just as their children are entitled to reasonable adjustments in the classroom. This right is not always communicated, and exercising it requires some preparation.

Practical adjustments that can be requested before a meeting: a room with natural or adjustable lighting rather than full fluorescent; a quieter space away from corridor noise; adequate water provided; permission to take written notes rather than produce verbal-only responses; confirmation that meeting documents will be circulated in advance; and agreement that any decisions requiring parental consent will be given time for the parent to consider before responding.

Some of these adjustments are harder to obtain than others depending on the school and the region. The ones worth prioritizing are the ones that most directly affect your ability to function: lighting if you have significant auditory sensitivity, advance documents if your processing is significantly slowed under social pressure, and time-to-decide protections if your RSD means you agree to things in the moment that do not serve your child.

If you disclose your own neurodivergence diagnosis to the school, you may be entitled to formal reasonable adjustments under disability legislation depending on your region. This is a personal decision. Some AuDHD parents find that disclosure is received positively and produces genuine accommodation. Others find that it shifts the dynamic in ways that are not helpful to their child's advocacy. The decision should be made based on your knowledge of the specific school and staff involved.

When Home Education Becomes the Answer

For some PDA children, school attendance becomes impossible regardless of the quality of school advocacy. The demand load of institutional education, even with significant adjustments, can exceed the capacity of a PDA nervous system. When this happens, home education may become the most viable option.

For an AuDHD parent, this presents a specific challenge: the standard advice about home education tends to assume a high degree of planning capacity, structured curriculum delivery, and consistent routine. These are exactly the executive function domains that ADHD impairs.

The good news is that home education for PDA children does not follow the standard model and actually cannot. PDA children do not respond to structured curriculum delivery any more than they respond to structured classroom delivery. The educational approach that works for PDA learners is autonomy-led, interest-following, and low-demand in structure, which means that the AuDHD parent who cannot maintain a rigid timetable is not failing to deliver good home education. They are, potentially, delivering the kind of education that actually works for their child.

Research on self-directed education and anxiety-driven school refusal has found that child-led approaches to learning outside formal schooling produce better outcomes for children with high anxiety and demand-sensitive profiles than curriculum-based home education models, primarily because they reduce the demand load to a level the child's nervous system can tolerate (Gray et al,, 2023).

Practically, home education for the AuDHD parent looks like this. The structure that exists is minimal and follows the child's interest: if they want to spend three weeks on one topic, that is the topic. The parent's role is to provide resources, facilitate access to materials, and create conditions where learning can happen rather than to deliver instruction. Deregistering from school and accessing the legal framework for home education in your region is the first practical step, and the requirements vary significantly by country and region.

The ADHD parent who worries about not being organized enough to home educate a child should know that home education of a PDA child is significantly less organized than any alternative model. That is not a bug. That is how it works.

Consider Godric (name changed), introduced in Chapter 3.0, whose daughter was unable to sustain school attendance beyond three days per week even with an individualized plan in place. When he moved to home education, he expected to feel more in control and more capable of managing her education. What actually happened was the opposite: she led entirely. She became absorbed in one interest area for months at a time. She designed her own project schedules, which she then revised constantly. She learned things he had not taught her. His role was largely to stay nearby, keep the house stocked with materials, and avoid introducing external demands into her learning space. He describes it as the most effective parenting he has done and the hardest, because it required radical acceptance of an approach that looked, from the outside, nothing like education, and everything like a child finally getting to be herself.

What Comes Next

The advocacy tools in this chapter apply primarily to formal institutional contexts. Chapter 7.0 addresses the daily rhythms of life in the double-ND household: how to build routines that are flexible enough for a PDA nervous system and consistent enough to support an ADHD parent who needs anchors to function.

The key takeaway from this chapter to carry forward is that preparation is the primary strategy for managing high-demand institutional contexts. The meeting you prepare for thoroughly is a different meeting from the one you walk into cold. And the advocacy that is written down in advance is available under pressure in a way that advocacy that has to be generated in the moment is not.

Essential Points

School meetings activate multiple AuDHD-specific difficulty areas simultaneously: the demand load of required attendance and engagement, the sensory challenges of institutional environments, the working memory demands of real-time complex discussion, and the RSD risk when the child's needs are disputed or minimized.

Preparation is the primary strategy. Five preparation steps reduce the in-meeting cognitive load significantly: obtaining the agenda in advance, identifying three to five key outcomes, preparing held-ground responses to anticipated resistance, deciding in advance what cannot be agreed to in the meeting, and managing the sensory environment proactively.

Pre-prepared advocacy scripts for common contested situations make factual, held-ground responses available under pressure without requiring in-the-moment generation.

Bringing a neurotypical ally to high-stakes meetings is a practical and legitimate strategy, not a failure of self-advocacy.

Home education for PDA children does not require the structured curriculum delivery that standard home education models assume. Autonomy-led, low-demand approaches produce better outcomes for PDA learners, which means the AuDHD parent's limited executive function for structure is not a disqualification. It may be an advantage.

Chapter 7.0 Daily Life Meals Hygiene and Routines for Two ND Brains

The Household That Has to Work Differently

Every household has rhythms. The way mornings unfold. The pattern of meals. The unspoken agreement about when the day ends and sleep begins. In most households, these rhythms develop through a combination of habit, social convention, and the path of least resistance. In the double-ND household, the path of least resistance runs through different terrain entirely.

The PDA child's nervous system does not respond to imposed schedules. Routine that arrives as demand activates avoidance. The ADHD parent's nervous system does not sustain imposed structure reliably, because the cognitive and motivational resources required to maintain a fixed schedule are precisely the ones that ADHD depletes fastest. Autistic sensory needs in both the parent and the child mean that the ordinary textures, smells, sounds, and temperatures of household life are not neutral background. They are active and requiring.

Standard advice about household routines assumes neurotypical participants on both sides of the parent-child dynamic. Visual schedules, reward systems, fixed mealtimes, and structured bedtime routines are the standard toolkit. For the double-ND household, this toolkit either does not work or actively makes things worse.

This chapter is about building the rhythms that do work. Not perfect routines. Not the household you imagined you would run. The household that can actually function, day after day, with the brains and nervous systems present.

Why Standard Routines Fail This Household

Before looking at what works, it is worth being precise about why standard approaches fail, because the failure is instructive.

Imposed routines fail PDA children because they represent a continuous demand load. The structure of a routine, the expectation that a specific thing will happen at a specific time regardless of the child's current state, is experienced by the PDA nervous system as a threat to autonomy. The child who refused breakfast at eight this morning is not being difficult. Their nervous system registered the expectation of breakfast at eight as a demand, and demand avoidance activated. The more consistently the routine is imposed, the more reliably the avoidance will appear in response.

Research on demand avoidance and routine in PDA profiles has found that rigid routine structures consistently produce higher rates of avoidance behavior than flexible, child-responsive approaches, because the rigidity of the routine eliminates the child's felt sense of control over their own day (Newson et al., 2003). The paradox for parents is that routines exist to create predictability, which should reduce anxiety. For PDA children, the predictability of what is going to be demanded of them increases, not decreases, the anxiety response.

For the ADHD parent, the failure mode is different but equally structural. Fixed routines require consistent initiation, time tracking, and sequential task completion at specified intervals. These are precisely the executive function skills that ADHD most reliably impairs. Research on time blindness in ADHD has found that ADHD adults have significantly impaired internal time perception, meaning they cannot reliably sense how much time has passed or how much time remains, and that this impairment is involuntary and does not improve substantially with motivation alone (Barkley, 2012). A mealtime that requires the parent to track that it has been four hours since the last meal, initiate a new sequence of food preparation, and deliver it at a consistent time each day is dependent on a time-sensing capacity that the ADHD parent may simply not have.

The solution is not to try harder at standard routines. It is to build something different from the ground up.

Flexible Structure: What It Actually Looks Like

Flexible structure is not the absence of structure. It is structure that bends in response to the state of the people inside it rather than remaining fixed regardless of that state.

The difference is between a rule and an anchor. A rule says: we eat at noon. An anchor says: we eat when the food is ready and people are available and the sensory conditions are manageable. The anchor points toward the same general territory as the rule. It does not prescribe the exact location.

Practically, flexible structure in the double-ND household is built from anchors rather than timetables. The day has recognizable shapes, loose beginning-middle-end rhythms, natural transition points that are indicated rather than demanded. These shapes are predictable enough to reduce anxiety and loose enough to accommodate the variability in both the parent's and the child's state on any given day.

The PDA child needs to know roughly what the day contains without having a fixed sequence imposed on them. A visual overview posted somewhere neutral, not handed to them as a schedule they must follow but simply available as information they can consult if they choose, provides this. It tells them the shape of the day without making compliance a demand. This approach draws on the distinction between information and instruction that underpins declarative language: the child can use the information or not. The availability of the information is the accommodation.

The ADHD parent needs anchors that do not depend on internal time tracking. Environmental cues rather than clock-watching: the light changing in the late afternoon, a specific alarm that signals an upcoming transition, a natural break in the child's activity that creates an opening. The parent who has learned to use environmental signals rather than internal time tracking is working with their ADHD rather than against it.

Consider Bramwell (name changed), a parent introduced in the Introduction as someone who reads books in non-linear chunks. His household with his PDA-profiled daughter runs almost entirely on environmental anchors rather than clock time. Mealtimes happen when someone is hungry and the sensory conditions in the kitchen are workable. The signal for approaching bedtime is not a clock but the natural wind-down in the household's activity level after the evening meal. His daughter knows these patterns not because they were imposed on her but because she has lived inside them long enough that they are familiar. She can predict roughly what the day will contain without being told what she has to do. Bramwell describes the household as one where no one is fighting the schedule because there is no schedule to fight. What exists instead is a loose rhythm that both of them have quietly agreed to through repeated experience rather than explicit negotiation.

Food: Aversions, ARFID, and Mealtimes That Work

Food in the double-ND household is often one of the most consistent sources of daily difficulty. Both autism and ADHD are associated with atypical food relationships that go well beyond preference. Many autistic people have significant sensory sensitivities to food textures, temperatures, smells, and appearances that make the ordinary concept of a balanced diet functionally inaccessible. ADHD is associated with irregular hunger signaling, impulsive food choices, and difficulty with meal initiation and planning.

When the child also has a PDA profile, mealtimes carry the additional demand load of expectation. The expectation that the child will eat, will sit at the table, will eat what has been prepared, and will do so at a specified time represents multiple stacked demands. Any one of them can trigger avoidance. Together they can make mealtimes a reliable daily crisis.

Avoidant Restrictive Food Intake Disorder, often abbreviated as ARFID, describes a pattern of food restriction based on sensory sensitivity, fear of aversive outcomes, or lack of interest in eating, rather than body image concerns. Research on ARFID and autism has found that ARFID-type presentations are significantly more common in autistic populations than in the general population and that they co-occur at particularly high rates with demand-sensitive and anxiety-driven profiles (Dumont-Mathieu & Fein, 2005). When both the parent and the child have ARFID-type food relationships, the household's food environment is shaped by two sets of genuine sensory and physiological needs rather than one.

What tends to work in this context is a food environment built around access rather than prescription. Food that is safe for both the parent and the child is available and accessible throughout the day rather than prepared and presented at fixed mealtimes. Meals that the parent is also willing to eat remove the sensory mismatch that arises when the parent cooks something they find aversive and expects the child to eat it. The table as a required location for eating can be dropped entirely if table-based eating consistently produces demand activation in the child. Eating in a comfortable sensory location, at a self-chosen time, with food that is genuinely tolerable to the child's sensory profile, is more nourishing than the nutritionally optimal meal that does not get eaten.

This does not mean nutrition is abandoned. It means the definition of a successful meal is recalibrated. A child with ARFID who ate a safe food in a comfortable location is better nourished than a child with ARFID who spent forty minutes at a table in a state of distress and ate nothing.

Consider Ivor (name changed), introduced in Chapter 3.0, who had significant food texture aversions and whose son's PDA profile meant that mealtime expectations triggered daily avoidance. Ivor eventually dismantled the concept of a family mealtime entirely. A range of safe foods for both of them is available in the kitchen throughout the day. His son eats when he is hungry, selects from available options, and eats wherever in the house his sensory state is most manageable. Ivor eats in a similar pattern. They sometimes eat in the same space and sometimes do not. From the outside, a professional observing would describe the household as having no mealtime structure. From the inside, both people are eating regularly and without the daily crisis that structured mealtimes consistently produced. Ivor reports that his son's relationship with food has become markedly less anxious since the demand of the mealtime was removed.

Hygiene Without Power Struggles

Personal hygiene is one of the most consistent flashpoints in PDA households. The demand to wash, brush teeth, change clothing, or shower is experienced by the PDA child's nervous system as both a direct demand and, frequently, a sensory demand. The combination is potent.

For many autistic children, hygiene tasks carry genuine sensory challenges. The temperature and pressure of water, the texture and smell of soap and shampoo, the sound of a shower, the sensation of toothbrush bristles on gums: these are not trivial discomforts. They are real sensory experiences that can be genuinely painful or overwhelming for a nervous system with atypical sensory processing. Adding the demand load of being told to endure those sensory experiences on a fixed schedule is the combination most likely to produce sustained avoidance and escalation.

The low-demand approach to hygiene works on two levels simultaneously. First, it reduces the demand structure around hygiene tasks. This means offering rather than directing, making hygiene resources available rather than initiating hygiene sequences, and removing the fixed schedule in favor of flexible timing. "The shower is free" is information. "You need to shower now" is a demand. "I notice it's been a while since you showered" is still, functionally, a demand dressed differently. The cleaner version is simply the shower being available, warm, and stocked with sensory-tolerable products, with no comment made.

Second, it addresses the sensory challenges within the task itself. This means finding sensory-safe products for the specific child: fragrance-free shampoo, soft-bristle toothbrushes, specific water temperatures, clothing that does not trigger skin sensitivity. These accommodations are not indulgence. They are the difference between a hygiene task that is physically manageable and one that is genuinely aversive.

Research on sensory processing and hygiene refusal in autistic children has found that sensory-adapted hygiene environments, using child-selected products and child-controlled timing and temperature, significantly reduced hygiene avoidance behaviors compared to standard demand-based approaches (Pfeiffer et al., 2011). The child who refuses to shower is very often refusing a sensory experience that their nervous system finds genuinely difficult, not simply refusing the demand for its own sake.

For the AuDHD parent, modeling without instructing can be a useful tool. Stating your own hygiene intention as information rather than as an implicit invitation for the child to mirror it: "I'm going to take a shower before we go" is information the child can use or ignore. It is not a demand that they do the same. Over time, many PDA children begin to self-initiate hygiene tasks on their own timelines when the demand around those tasks has been consistently absent.

Consider Crispin (name changed), introduced in Chapter 1.0, who spent two years in daily conflict with his daughter over shower resistance before shifting his approach entirely. He stopped mentioning it. He kept the bathroom stocked with the specific products she preferred. He occasionally stated his own intention to shower, with no reference to whether she would do the same. Within three months, his daughter had begun showering independently, at her own chosen times, without any mention of it. He does not fully understand the mechanism. He understands that removing the demand removed the avoidance, and that the hygiene is now happening reliably without any input from him.

Sleep When Nobody Is Tired at Bedtime

Sleep is the area where PDA parenting guides most consistently offer advice that does not translate to the double-ND household. Standard guidance recommends consistent bedtimes, wind-down routines, screens-off before sleep, and age-appropriate sleep hours. These recommendations are not wrong for the populations they are designed for. They simply do not function in a household where the child's PDA means bedtime is a demand-saturated event and the parent's ADHD means their own sleep regulation is also atypical.

Many autistic people have a delayed sleep phase, meaning their natural sleep onset time is significantly later than the conventional social norm (Díaz-Morales & Escribano, 2015). Many ADHD adults have similar sleep phase irregularities combined with hyperactivation of the mind at what conventional society defines as bedtime. The child who cannot fall asleep at nine o'clock and the parent who cannot either are not being non-compliant with sleep. They are running their neurological sleep programs, which happen to operate on a different schedule.

The rigid bedtime routine is, for the PDA child, a daily cascade of demands: stop doing what you are doing, go to this specific room, lie in this specific position, do not speak, do not move, and go to sleep. The PDA nervous system's response to this demand sequence is predictable: resistance, escalation, and a stress response that makes sleep even less likely.

What tends to work instead is a sleep environment rather than a sleep routine. This means the conditions of the sleep space are comfortable and sensory-tolerable, the transition toward sleep is gradual and indicated rather than demanded, and the timing is guided by biological readiness rather than clock. Dim lighting in the evening shifts the light environment toward sleep naturally. Low-demand activities that the child can engage in independently in bed, reading, listening to audio, drawing, allow the nervous system to settle without a specific transition being demanded. A natural wind-down that follows the evening's activities creates the conditions for sleep without announcing that sleep is now required.

The parent's own sleep requires the same non-coercive approach. The ADHD adult who tries to force sleep at a conventional time by lying down and doing nothing is setting themselves up for hyperactivation rather than sleep onset. Low-demand wind-down activities that allow the mind to settle, audio content, gentle movement, environmental sensory management, work better than strict sleep hygiene prescriptions that ignore the neurology they are being applied to.

Consider Oswin (name changed), introduced in Chapter 4.0, whose daughter consistently resisted bedtime until the demand structure was entirely removed. Oswin replaced the bedtime routine with an evening rhythm: the lights in the house shifted to lamp-only after the evening meal, the auditory environment became quieter and slower, her daughter had access to quiet activities in her room from mid-evening, and there was no specified time by which she needed to be asleep. Her daughter's sleep onset shifted earlier over several weeks, not because sleep was demanded but because the environmental conditions made sleep the path of least resistance. She still goes to sleep later than conventionally recommended for her age. She goes to sleep significantly earlier than she did when bedtime was a daily battle.

Creating Household Rhythms That Bend Without Breaking

The household rhythm that works for the double-ND household is one that has predictable shapes without fixed timings, familiar sequences without enforced compliance, and enough flexibility to absorb the high-variability days without collapsing entirely.

Building this rhythm is not a one-time design project. It is an ongoing process of noticing what works and what generates unnecessary conflict, and gradually shifting the household's patterns toward more of the former and less of the latter. This is itself a form of pattern recognition, the same skill identified in Chapter 1.0 as one of the AuDHD parent's genuine strengths in this context.

Some principles that tend to hold across different double-ND households. Predictability in the shape of the day matters more than precision in its timing. The child who knows that the day contains a meal, some free time, some connection with the parent, and an eventual wind toward sleep is less anxious than the child who does not know what to expect, regardless of whether those elements occur at exactly the same time each day.

Transitions are the highest-risk points. Not because transitions are intrinsically difficult for PDA children, but because transitions are demand-dense moments in most households. They can be made lower-demand by indication rather than instruction, by advance information rather than sudden announcement, and by allowing more transition time than seems necessary. The child who is told the transition is coming fifteen minutes before it arrives is in a different state from the child who is told to stop what they are doing immediately.

The parent's own consistency matters less than their predictability. An ADHD parent who cannot maintain the same behavior every day can still maintain recognizable patterns that the child can rely on. The parent who sometimes responds in one way and sometimes in another is more dysregulating for a PDA child than a parent whose responses are somewhat inconsistent in execution but consistent in underlying approach. The underlying approach, low-demand, relationally safe, flexible but present, is what the child's nervous system is tracking.

Essential Points

Standard household routines fail the double-ND household for structural reasons. PDA neurology reads imposed routine as continuous demand. ADHD neurology struggles to maintain fixed schedules reliably. Both failures are predictable and neither is a personal failing.

Flexible structure built from anchors rather than timetables serves both neurotypes. Anchors indicate the shape of the day without prescribing compliance. Environmental cues replace clock-watching for the ADHD parent. Informational visibility of the day's shape reduces PDA anxiety without imposing demand.

Food in the double-ND household works best as access rather than prescription. ARFID-type presentations require sensory-responsive food environments rather than nutritional compliance frameworks. The meal that gets eaten in a comfortable setting is more nourishing than the optimal meal that is refused.

Hygiene without power struggles requires removing both the demand structure and the sensory obstacles. Sensory-adapted products, child-controlled timing, and parental modeling without instruction are the practical tools.

Sleep works better as an environment than a routine. Gradual environmental shifts toward sleep conditions, low-demand evening activity access, and biological rather than clock-based timing all serve the double-ND household better than imposed bedtime sequences.

Household rhythms that bend without breaking are built from predictable shapes, generous transition time, and consistency in underlying approach rather than consistency in specific execution.

Chapter 8.0 Your Late Diagnosis Grief Identity and Reparenting Yourself

The News That Arrives Too Late

For most AuDHD adults who receive their diagnosis in midlife, the news arrives in a specific emotional sequence. First, recognition. Then relief, often immediately followed by confusion about the relief. Then, sometime after the initial processing, something that feels uncomfortably like grief.

The grief is real, and it is not always named as grief in the clinical or social frameworks around late diagnosis. It tends to be described instead as adjustment, or processing, or coming to terms with. These phrases are not wrong but they are insufficient. What late-diagnosed AuDHD adults are often grieving is not just the absence of a label. They are grieving the years lived without understanding. The strategies that cost them enormously and might not have been necessary with different support. The relationships that failed for reasons they could not name. The careers that did not happen, the exhaustion that was attributed to character, the constant low-level sense of being inadequate at something that other people seemed to manage without effort.

For the AuDHD parent who discovers their own neurotype in the context of their child's PDA diagnosis, this grief arrives alongside a specific additional dimension: the realization that some of what they struggled with as a child was the same thing their child is now struggling with. And that the responses they received, the strategies that were tried on them, the ways their behavior was interpreted and addressed, were built on a fundamental misunderstanding of what was actually happening in their nervous system.

This chapter is about the emotional and identity work of late diagnosis as it intersects with active parenting. It does not ask you to put the grief down before it is ready to be put down. It asks you to carry it in a way that allows you to also be present for your child, and to find in the processing of your own experience the material for something that is actually useful.

What Late Diagnosis Grief Involves

Late diagnosis grief is not a single coherent emotion. It is a cluster of often contradictory experiences that tend to arrive at different times and sometimes simultaneously.

There is often a version of relief that feels inappropriate: how can I feel relieved about a diagnosis? Relief arrives because the diagnostic label provides a framework for experiences that were previously inexplicable. The years of inexplicable exhaustion. The social situations that went wrong in ways no one could explain. The executive function failures that looked to everyone including yourself like simple laziness or irresponsibility. The label does not change any of those experiences, but it changes how they are interpreted. Interpreted differently, they become less evidence of fundamental deficiency and more evidence of a nervous system operating under conditions it was not built for without adequate support.

There is often anger. The anger tends to have multiple targets: the diagnostic systems that missed it, the educational institutions that responded to the symptoms rather than the cause, the caregivers who could not provide what was needed because they did not know what was needed, and sometimes the self, for not having known sooner. The anger is legitimate at all of these targets and does not require resolution before the other work can happen.

There is often a disorienting experience of identity reorganization. The narrative of the self, accumulated over decades of living as an undiagnosed person, is built on certain interpretations: this is who I am, this is what I am capable of, this is why things went wrong, this is what is wrong with me. Late diagnosis disrupts every one of those interpretations simultaneously. The reorganization that follows can feel like losing solid ground rather than gaining it, at least initially. This is disorienting. It is also, eventually, one of the most significant pieces of psychological work available to a late-diagnosed person.

Research on the psychological impact of late autism diagnosis in adults has found that while many late-diagnosed people report improved wellbeing over time following diagnosis, the initial period is frequently characterized by significant distress, identity disruption, and re-processing of past experiences through a new interpretive lens (Huang et al., 2020). The distress is not a sign that the diagnosis was a mistake. It is the expected output of a major reinterpretation of a decades-long personal history.

Consider Jory (name changed), introduced in Chapter 2.0, who received her AuDHD diagnosis in her late thirties, several years after her daughter's PDA profile was identified. Jory describes the first year after her diagnosis as one of the most disorienting of her life, which she finds uncomfortable to admit because she had been expecting it to feel like finally having answers. Answers arrived. But alongside them came a sustained process of reviewing her life and finding, repeatedly, moments where the absence of a diagnosis had meant the absence of appropriate support. The job she had left because she could not sustain the sensory load and had assumed she was not resilient enough. The relationship that had ended because her communication style was repeatedly misinterpreted as coldness. The years of therapy that had addressed symptoms without ever naming the underlying cause. She does not regret those years. She grieves them in a specific way that is different from regret: she knows now what was needed then, and she knows it was not available to her, and that knowledge sits in a particular place in her chest that takes some time to become workable.

When Your Child Surfaces Your Unresolved Wounds

Parenting a PDA child while carrying unprocessed late-diagnosis material is not simply a matter of two separate challenges happening at the same time. They interact. The child's experience of demand avoidance, of having their needs dismissed by institutions, of being told their behavior is a choice when it is a neurological response, can activate the parent's own memories of the same experiences in ways that are immediate, visceral, and not always recognizable as memories.

This phenomenon has a name in clinical literature. Intergenerational trauma refers to the transmission of trauma-related patterns across generations, and it has been documented in populations where similar experiences repeat between parent and child (Yehuda & Lehrner, 2018). In the context of late-diagnosed AuDHD parents of PDA children, the mechanism is somewhat different but the dynamic is recognizable: the parent's unprocessed experiences of being misunderstood, over-demanded, and unsupported activate in the presence of their child's similar experiences. The parent's emotional response to the child's situation may be much larger than the immediate situation alone would produce, because it carries the weight of their own accumulated history.

This is important to understand because it affects how the parent is able to respond in the moment. A parent who is watching their child's meltdown and is simultaneously re-experiencing the memory of their own childhood meltdowns without the support they needed is not in a position to provide optimal co-regulation. Their threat response is carrying two loads. Their capacity to stay regulated in the face of the child's distress is reduced not by insufficient love but by the weight of unprocessed experience that the situation is activating.

The practical implication is not that the parent must resolve all their childhood material before they can parent effectively. That would be an unreasonable standard and a misunderstanding of how therapy and healing actually work. The practical implication is that identifying the specific triggers that activate the parent's own history is useful clinical and personal information, and that having some of that awareness allows for a slightly different response in the moment: not just this is my child's distress, but this is also resonating with something of mine, and I can hold both of those things separately.

Consider Merrick (name changed), introduced in Chapter 4.0, who has an AuDHD diagnosis and whose son has a PDA profile. Merrick grew up in a household where his need for predictability and his sensory sensitivity were consistently framed as difficulty. He was described as oversensitive, inflexible, and demanding. His late diagnosis at thirty-eight provided a framework for understanding what had actually been happening during those years. What he did not initially anticipate was the degree to which watching his son be told by teachers that his avoidance was a behavior choice would activate his own specific memory of being told the same thing. He began to notice that his most dysregulated responses to his son's school-related difficulties were not primarily about his son. They were about him, at nine years old, being told his behavior was a choice. Understanding the source did not remove the activation. But it gave him a way to name what was happening that made it slightly more manageable: this is mine, not just his. I can deal with mine separately.

The Grief of the Childhood That Could Have Been

There is a specific form of grief that many late-diagnosed AuDHD parents of neurodivergent children describe, and it is worth naming directly because it is rarely discussed in the literature on late diagnosis.

It is the grief of watching your child receive the support you did not have.

This grief is complicated. There is something in it that looks like jealousy and is not jealousy. It is closer to the feeling of watching a wound on someone else being treated properly and knowing, for the first time, that yours also needed treatment and did not receive it. There is often a gratitude inside this grief: your child is getting what they need. There is also, alongside the gratitude, a quiet awareness of what the absence of that support cost you and what it might have been like to grow up differently.

This grief does not require resolution before you can provide good support to your child. Many parents carry it indefinitely alongside their parenting, and it does not prevent effective parenting. What it can interfere with is the capacity to stay present in moments that closely mirror the parent's own childhood experiences of unsupported neurodivergence. In those moments, the grief can produce a response that belongs to the parent's past rather than the child's present.

The work of late diagnosis grief, to the extent that work is the right word for something that is more like a gradual metabolizing, is the slow process of recontextualizing past experiences without either dismissing their impact or being overwhelmed by them. This is, fundamentally, the work of self-compassion described in Chapter 4.0, but applied across a longer timeline and a deeper layer of history.

Reparenting Yourself While Parenting Them

Reparenting is a concept from various therapeutic traditions that refers to the process of providing for yourself, in the present, some of what was not provided in childhood. This might mean learning to recognize your own sensory needs and respond to them without shame. It might mean developing the self-compassion that was not modeled or offered to you when you were a child. It might mean building the understanding of your own nervous system that you are simultaneously building for your child.

For AuDHD parents of PDA children, reparenting has a specific and concrete form: the work of understanding your own neurotype is simultaneously the work of understanding your child's. The things you learn about demand avoidance apply to your past experience as well as your child's current one. The accommodations you make for your child's sensory needs are the same accommodations you might legitimately make for your own.

This creates a kind of dual movement. As the parent learns to respond to the child's PDA profile with a lower-demand approach, they are also, often for the first time, learning to respond to their own historical demand sensitivity with something other than shame and forced compliance. As the parent develops compassion for the child's difficulty with transitions, they are also, often for the first time, developing permission to have difficulty with transitions themselves.

Research on self-compassion and parenting outcomes has found that parents who score higher on self-compassion measures demonstrate more responsive, less controlling, and more emotionally attuned parenting behaviors, and that this effect is particularly pronounced in parents with histories of childhood adversity (Neff & McGehee, 2010). The dual healing journey, doing for yourself what you are doing for your child, is not a distraction from parenting. It is one of the most direct routes to better parenting outcomes available.

The practical form of reparenting for the AuDHD parent is less dramatic than the concept sometimes suggests. It looks like: noticing when you are applying to yourself the same harsh standards that were applied to you as a child, and making a deliberate adjustment toward something more accurate. It looks like: recognizing your own sensory needs as real and legitimate rather than inconvenient. It looks like: building the environmental structures that your childhood home did not provide, not to recreate a childhood but to function better in the present. And it looks like: extending to your past self the understanding you are extending to your child, that the behavior that looked like defiance or failure was the output of a nervous system doing what nervous systems do under the conditions it was given.

Consider Dunstan (name changed), introduced in Chapter 2.0 and Chapter 6.0, who was raised in a household with what he now recognizes as high demand density and little understanding of neurodivergent needs. His late diagnosis arrived when his younger child's PDA profile was being assessed. The reparenting work that followed was not, for Dunstan, a therapeutic project he undertook deliberately. It was more like a series of involuntary recognitions that accumulated over time. Watching his younger child be assessed for PDA, he kept identifying items on the assessment that described his own childhood. Watching his child's specialist explain demand sensitivity to him, he kept recognizing the explanations as descriptions of what he had been told was pure stubbornness or bad attitude. The reparenting was the slow replacement of those old interpretations with the new framework, applied not just to his present self but to his past self sitting in classrooms and at dinner tables and in the headteacher's office, being told things about himself that were not accurate.

Building a Neurodivergent Identity Without Losing Parenting Momentum

Late diagnosis offers something that is easy to underestimate while you are in the grief of it: it offers a new and more accurate framework for self-understanding. The identity work of late diagnosis is the process of constructing a self-narrative that incorporates the new information without either collapsing into it or dismissing it.

For AuDHD parents, the risk on one side is of becoming so absorbed in the identity work that the parenting suffers. There is a version of late-diagnosis processing that becomes the central organizing project of the parent's life to the exclusion of the relationships and responsibilities that also require attention. This is understandable. Decades of unidentified neurodivergence produce a significant backlog of experiences that need recontextualization. But parenting a PDA child in active need is not on pause while the parent does that work.

The risk on the other side is of suppressing the identity work entirely in service of the parenting demands. This tends not to work in the medium term. Unprocessed late-diagnosis material does not disappear. It surfaces in the situations described earlier in this chapter: the moments when the child's experience activates the parent's own history, the moments when the grief arrives without warning in the middle of an ordinary Tuesday.

The middle path is an integration that allows both to coexist. The parent who is doing their late-diagnosis identity work is not failing to parent. The parent who is fully present for their child's difficult moment is not failing to process their own history. These can and do happen at the same time, not always cleanly and not always with the emotional tidiness that therapeutic frameworks sometimes suggest, but sustainably and with accumulating effect.

Neurodivergent community is one of the most consistently reported resources for late-diagnosed adults navigating identity formation. Research on the experiences of autistic adults who discovered their diagnosis in adulthood found that connection with other autistic adults was one of the most significant predictors of positive post-diagnosis adjustment, more so than therapy or medication alone (Crane et al., 2019). For AuDHD parents, this means communities of other late-diagnosed AuDHD parents, ideally those who are also raising neurodivergent children, offer something that professional support alone cannot: the felt sense of being accurately recognized by people who are navigating similar terrain.

What Comes Next

The work in this chapter is less linear than the practical content in earlier chapters. Late diagnosis grief, identity formation, intergenerational wound recognition, and reparenting are not tasks to be completed before moving to the next chapter. They are ongoing processes that develop alongside the daily work of parenting.

Chapter 9.0 addresses the co-parenting and relationship dimensions of the double-ND household: what happens when partners have different neurotypes, when one parent receives a diagnosis and the other does not, and how the stress of raising a PDA child affects relationships that were not designed for the intensity they are carrying.

The one thing to hold from this chapter before turning to that one: the grief and identity work of late diagnosis is not a detour from parenting. It is part of the same project. Understanding yourself more accurately makes you a better parent to your child. And the compassion you develop for your own late-identified needs is the same compassion you bring to your child's currently identified needs. The two journeys are not parallel. They are intertwined.

Essential Points

Late diagnosis grief is real, it is not always named as grief, and it involves relief, anger, identity disruption, and the specific grief of knowing what was needed and not received in childhood.

The parent's child surfaces unresolved material because the child's neurodivergent experiences can directly activate the parent's own historical experiences. Understanding the source of disproportionate emotional responses in parenting moments, recognizing this is mine, not just theirs, is clinically useful and practically important.

The grief of watching your child receive support you did not have is one of the least-discussed forms of late diagnosis grief. It does not need to be resolved to allow effective parenting, but it benefits from being named.

Reparenting, in its practical form, is the application of the same neurodivergent-affirming framework you are building for your child to your own past and present experience. The dual healing journey is not a distraction from parenting. Research supports it as one of the more direct routes to improved parenting outcomes.

Building a neurodivergent identity alongside active parenting does not require choosing one over the other. The integration of identity work and parenting is sustainable and accumulates over time.

Chapter 9.0 Partners Co-Parents and the Extended Family Minefield

The Household in a Wider World

Every family exists inside a larger social context. Parents, siblings, in-laws, school staff, neighbors, the pediatrician who has known the child since birth: these relationships form the outer layer of any household's life. For most families, the outer layer is a resource. A source of backup childcare, practical advice, emotional support, and the general sense of not being alone in the project of raising children.

For the double-ND household raising a PDA child, the outer layer is frequently more complicated than that. The parenting approach required by a PDA profile runs so counter to cultural norms around discipline, structure, and compliance that the adults closest to the family often become sources of pressure rather than support. The grandparent who notices the child does not comply with instructions and concludes the parents need to be firmer. The co-parent who has read different books and arrives at weekends with a behavioral reward chart. The well-meaning sibling who asks why the child is allowed to eat wherever they want in the house.

And underneath all of that, the specific difficulty of the AuDHD parent navigating social conflict. The autistic preference for directness that can come across as aggression in family conversations. The ADHD impulsivity that means the response to an unwanted comment arrives before its consequences have been considered. The RSD that makes criticism of your parenting feel like an acute physical event rather than a difference of opinion. The emotional exhaustion that means the cognitive bandwidth required for diplomatic family navigation is often simply not available.

This chapter addresses the relational outer layer of the double-ND household. It does not offer a blueprint for managing all families. It offers tools for the specific combination of challenges that face the AuDHD parent navigating neurotypical relationships while parenting a PDA child.

When Your Co-Parent Does Not Get It

Co-parenting with someone who does not share your understanding of your child's PDA profile is one of the most consistently reported challenges among parents of PDA children, and the challenge is substantially amplified when the understanding parent is also navigating their own AuDHD in a relationship with someone who does not share that neurotype.

The difficulty operates on multiple levels. At the most practical level, inconsistency between co-parents in the demand load they place on the child is genuinely problematic for the child's nervous system. A child who experiences a low-demand approach at home and a high-demand approach at a co-parent's household, or on weekends with the other parent, is not experiencing two different parenting philosophies. They are experiencing two different nervous system states repeatedly, without the consistency that allows the nervous system to build a stable baseline. Research on parenting consistency and anxiety in children with demand-sensitive profiles has found that inconsistency in demand levels across caregivers is associated with higher baseline anxiety and more frequent escalation events, because the child cannot predict which environment they are entering (Green et al., 2018).

At a relational level, the conflict between parenting approaches can become the site where wider relationship tensions accumulate. When one parent has read the PDA literature extensively and the other has not, when one parent has their own late-diagnosis processing underway and the other does not share that context, when one parent's nervous system is regularly activated by the parenting demands and the other is not, the disagreement about parenting approach can become a proxy for a wider and harder conversation.

The goal of co-parent communication about PDA is not to achieve agreement through superior argumentation. Most parenting disagreements that are resolved through one partner convincing the other produce surface agreement and underlying resentment rather than genuine shift. The more sustainable goal is shared observation: both parents observing the same child in similar situations and discussing what they notice, rather than one parent presenting a theory for the other to accept or reject.

This means finding specific, concrete examples rather than general principles. Not "PDA children need low-demand approaches" but "I noticed that last Tuesday when we told him directly to come to the table he escalated for forty minutes, and on Thursday when I just mentioned the food was ready and sat down, he came within five minutes." Specific observations are harder to dismiss than theoretical frameworks, particularly for partners who are skeptical of diagnostic labels or clinical language.

It also means acknowledging what is genuinely difficult about the low-demand approach from the other parent's perspective. The approach can look, from the outside, like the child is being given control of the household. The counter-argument is not that the child is not actually running the household, but that the PDA profile makes some of the standard tools of parenting actively counterproductive for this specific child, and that the observed data from your household supports this.

Consider Fenwick (name changed), introduced in Chapter 1.0, who described a period of approximately two years during which his low-demand approach to his son's PDA profile was a consistent point of conflict with his co-parent partner. His partner was neurotypical and held a strong belief that the approach was teaching their son that avoidance had no consequences. The breakthrough was not a book, a therapist, or a convincing argument. It was a shared observation over a half-term week when both parents were present every day. By the end of the week, his partner had noticed independently that direct instructions consistently produced longer and more intense escalations than informational statements. She had not been convinced of a theory. She had observed a consistent pattern in her own child and drawn her own conclusions. Fenwick describes the two weeks before that observation as the most tempted he had ever been to say "I told you so" and the most careful he had ever been not to say it.

Explaining the Double-ND Household to Extended Family

Grandparents, aunts, uncles, and close family friends represent a specific category of relational challenge that is distinct from co-parenting conflict. Their involvement is typically less frequent and therefore less immediately impactful, but their opinions often carry particular emotional weight for the parent, especially the parent who grew up in their household and carries the relational history of that.

The first thing to clarify, for yourself as much as for them, is what you need from extended family members. There are broadly three categories of need: to be understood, to be left alone to parent in your own way, and to receive practical support that is actually useful rather than destabilizing. These are different needs that require different conversations.

If what you need is to be understood, the conversation is educational. You are giving them information about PDA and about your child's profile specifically, with the goal of building enough comprehension that their interactions with your child cause less disruption. The challenge is that PDA is genuinely counterintuitive. Grandparents who raised children in an era of more explicit behavioral management often find the low-demand approach baffling at best and irresponsible at worst. The educational conversation is not likely to produce full comprehension in one sitting. It is a process that happens over multiple interactions and is probably most effective when it can be tied to specific observed moments with the child rather than delivered as abstract information.

If what you need is to be left alone to parent in your own way, the conversation is about boundary-setting rather than education. You are not asking for their agreement. You are informing them that you have made a specific parenting decision for specific reasons, and that the decision is not under review. This conversation is harder for many AuDHD adults than it sounds. The autistic preference for others to understand the reasoning behind decisions, combined with the vulnerability of having a parenting approach that is regularly challenged, can make it difficult to state a boundary without turning it into a justification that then becomes available for debate.

The useful framing is: "This is what works for our child. I'm not asking for agreement, but I do need our approach to be consistent when you're with the children." This states the practical requirement without opening a theoretical discussion. It may produce resistance. The resistance is data about the relationship, not an invitation to persuade.

If what you need is practical support that does not destabilize, the conversation is about specifics. Not "can you help sometimes" but "the specific help that works is this: being here on a Tuesday afternoon so I can have two hours alone. The specific help that doesn't work is giving our child direct instructions or introducing new expectations when you're with them."

Consider Larkin (name changed), introduced in Chapter 4.0, whose mother-in-law had strong opinions about her grandson's behavior and regularly offered unsolicited commentary during family visits. Larkin, who has a combined AuDHD profile with particular sensitivity to criticism of her parenting, had spent two years managing a low-grade anxiety about extended family visits that made the week before any family gathering almost uniformly exhausting. The change came not from a direct confrontation but from a specific conversation between Larkin and her partner about what was needed, followed by her partner having a single, clear conversation with his mother about what helpful support looked like and what made things harder. The conversation was not primarily about PDA. It was about practical parameters: please do not offer feedback on parenting decisions during visits; please do not give our son direct instructions; please do not ask him why he is behaving a certain way. These were specific, behavioral requests rather than educational asks. The mother-in-law's comprehension of PDA did not change significantly. Her behavior during visits did.

The "They Need More Discipline" Conversation

There is a version of this conversation that every parent of a PDA child has had. Someone in the outer circle, a family member, a family friend, occasionally a professional who does not understand PDA, observes the child's behavior and concludes that the root cause is insufficient structure, insufficient consequences, or insufficient parental authority. The solution they offer is some version of: be firmer, follow through, show them who is in charge.

This advice is not helpful. It is also not random. It reflects a coherent model of child behavior that is simply the wrong model for PDA profiles. Most child behavior management frameworks are built on the premise that children will do things they find aversive if the consequence of not doing them is more aversive still. For PDA children, this premise fails because the consequence-based demand is itself processed as a threat, which activates the avoidance response more strongly rather than less.

Increasing the firmness of a demand-based approach with a PDA child does not produce compliance. It produces escalation.

The difficulty of the "more discipline" conversation for the AuDHD parent is multiple. The autistic processing of social criticism often produces a stronger emotional response than the situation warrants cognitively. RSD means the implication that your parenting is inadequate can arrive with acute emotional force. ADHD impulsivity means the response arrives before its consequences have been considered. The combination of these three factors is a reliable recipe for a conversation that begins as an exchange of opinions and ends as a family incident.

Some practical tools for navigating this conversation. First, a pre-prepared response that does not invite debate: "We're working with a specialist who understands our child's specific neurological profile and we're following her recommendations." This states a fact, positions the parenting approach as professionally supported, and does not open a theoretical discussion. Most people will not argue with a specialist.

Second, the option to end the topic rather than the conversation: "I hear that you see it differently. We've made a decision about what works for our child, and it's not something I'm able to discuss right now." This is direct, it is not rude, and it closes the topic without requiring the other person to agree.

Third, the recognition that this conversation does not require resolution. You do not need the person offering unsolicited advice to understand your child's profile, agree with your parenting approach, or acknowledge that they were wrong. You need the conversation to end without a family rupture. Those are different goals and the second is more achievable.

Consider Ivor (name changed), introduced in Chapter 3.0, who encountered the "more discipline" argument from his brother at a family gathering. His brother had observed his son's refusal to sit at the dinner table and drawn the expected conclusion. Ivor, who had been doing the low-demand work for three years and whose son's outcomes had improved measurably, felt the familiar combination of exhaustion and outrage at having to justify an approach he knew was working. He used a version of the specialist framing and changed the subject. His brother did not become a convert to low-demand parenting. The dinner continued without incident. Ivor describes this as one of the more mature navigations of his adult life, not because he handled it brilliantly but because he recognized in the moment that the goal was continuation without rupture, not vindication.

Protecting the Family Unit from External Pressure

External pressure on the double-ND household is not limited to specific conversations with specific people. It is also structural: the accumulated weight of living inside a culture that does not understand PDA, does not accommodate neurodivergence generally, and consistently positions the double-ND household's adaptations as problems rather than appropriate responses to specific neurological realities.

This structural pressure cannot be resolved through individual conversations. It requires something more like a deliberate management of the household's relationship with the wider world. Who has access. How much access. What information is shared and with whom. Which relationships are worth the energy investment and which are not.

The concept of family boundary-setting is not new and not specific to neurodivergent families. What is specific to the double-ND household is the degree to which the boundary-setting work is expensive in precisely the resources that are most depleted: the executive function required to make and maintain consistent decisions, the emotional regulation required to communicate boundaries without either over-explaining or aggressing, and the self-trust required to protect an unconventional parenting approach against conventional social pressure.

Some relationships will not be compatible with the double-ND household's needs in their current form. This is not a failure. It is information. A grandparent who cannot modulate their behavior enough to avoid destabilizing the child's nervous system during visits may need to have less frequent or shorter visits. A sibling whose commentary on parenting consistently activates the parent's RSD may need to be seen less and in different contexts. An extended family gathering that reliably produces a three-day recovery may need to become optional rather than obligatory.

These decisions are not dramatic or permanent. They are calibrations made in the service of the household's functioning. The family unit that works is more important than the family calendar that satisfies everyone's expectations.

Navigating Neurotypical Co-Parenting Challenges

When the co-parenting partnership involves one neurodivergent parent and one neurotypical parent, the dynamic is not simply one of disagreement about strategy. It is a neurological mismatch in how each parent processes the demands of the household, recovers from high-intensity interactions, and experiences the daily stress of raising a PDA child.

The neurotypical co-parent may recover from a meltdown incident more quickly than the AuDHD co-parent. They may not experience the same cumulative sensory depletion from a day at home with a dysregulated child. They may not have the same threshold for when a given situation requires the low-demand approach rather than a direct request. These are not character differences. They are neurological differences, and they produce a consistent asymmetry in the parenting experience that, if unaddressed, tends to generate resentment on both sides.

The AuDHD parent who is more depleted after the same day of parenting may need more recovery time, more support, and more understanding of why certain strategies are non-negotiable. The neurotypical co-parent who does not experience the same depletion may struggle to understand why a strategy that seems merely inconvenient to them is genuinely inaccessible to their partner under stress.

The most useful intervention in this mismatch is explicit communication about state rather than implicit expectation of understanding. Not "you should know I'm depleted" but "I'm in a very depleted state right now and I need to hand the next hour to you." Not "you're making it harder" but "when you use that approach with him it usually means the evening takes longer to settle." Specific, state-based, present-tense communication is accessible to both neurotypes in a way that implied expectation is not.

Essential Points

Co-parenting disagreement about PDA approaches is best addressed through shared observation rather than theoretical persuasion. Specific, concrete examples of what produces escalation and what reduces it are harder to dismiss than clinical frameworks.

Extended family members generally need different things in different situations: some need education, some need clearly stated limits, and some need specific practical guidance about what helpful looks like and what is destabilizing. These are different conversations requiring different approaches.

The "more discipline" conversation does not require resolution or agreement. It requires an end without family rupture. Pre-prepared responses that do not invite debate, and the recognition that vindication is a different goal from continuation, are the practical tools.

Protecting the family unit from external pressure is not dramatic or permanent. It is calibration: which relationships can be invested in, which need to be modified in frequency or context, and which information is necessary to share and which is not.

Neurotypical and AuDHD co-parents experience the same parenting demands very differently. Explicit communication about state and capacity, rather than implicit expectation of understanding, is the most accessible communication format for both neurotypes.

Chapter 10.0 Burnout Compassion Fatigue and Sustainable Parenting

When Tired Is Not the Right Word

There is a kind of exhaustion that does not resolve with sleep. That accumulates across months in ways that are not always visible until something small tips the whole structure. That feels, from the inside, less like fatigue and more like a progressive narrowing of what is available: fewer words, less patience, less access to the strategies that usually work, less capacity to find the thing that usually helps. This is not ordinary tiredness. It has a different texture and a different cause, and it responds to different interventions.

For AuDHD parents of PDA children, this kind of exhaustion arrives more quickly, accumulates more silently, and is more easily misidentified than it is for neurotypical parents in similar situations. The autistic dimension means that the sensory and social processing demands of daily parenting in a high-intensity household are substantially higher than they appear from the outside. The ADHD dimension means that the compensatory strategies that mask depletion, increased effortful performance, caffeine, hyperfocus on a problem to delay the awareness of being overwhelmed, can sustain apparent functioning well past the point where genuine reserves have run out. The PDA dimension of the household means that the baseline demand load is structurally elevated, day after day, without the recovery windows that more straightforward households naturally provide.

The result is a burnout profile that is qualitatively different from neurotypical parental exhaustion, and that requires different recognition and different responses.

This chapter names what is happening with the precision it deserves. It also offers an honest account of what sustainable parenting actually looks like in the double-ND household, which is different from what most parenting self-care literature describes, and better calibrated to what is actually achievable.

Autistic Burnout: What It Is and How It Hides

Autistic burnout is not a metaphor for being very tired. It is a clinically recognized state that results from sustained masking and high-demand environments without adequate recovery, and its features are distinct from general fatigue or depression. Research on autistic burnout has described it as a state of chronic exhaustion, loss of skills, and reduced tolerance for stimulus, distinct from depression but frequently misdiagnosed as such, and resulting from the cumulative cost of operating in environments that do not accommodate the autistic nervous system (Raymaker et al., 2020).

The key features of autistic burnout that are important to recognize in the context of AuDHD parenting are these. First, skill regression: the autistic adult in burnout may lose access to communication skills, executive function capacities, and emotional regulation abilities that were previously available. Skills that appeared stable may become suddenly unavailable. This is not a personality change or a character failure. It is a neurological state.

Second, sensory sensitivity escalation: the sensory tolerance that was managing adequately may become insufficient. Sounds that were previously tolerable become intolerable. The tactile environment of the household, the noise level, the proximity of other people, becomes harder to sustain. This escalation of sensory sensitivity in the parent compounds directly with the sensory demands of a PDA household.

Third, the stealth quality of the onset. Autistic burnout often does not arrive suddenly. It builds across months through the progressive depletion of compensatory resources, and because the autistic adult has often spent decades learning to mask and perform adequacy regardless of internal state, the burnout may not be recognized by the person experiencing it until it is already severe.

In the context of parenting a PDA child, autistic burnout is particularly difficult to identify because the burnout symptoms, withdrawal, reduced communication, lower sensory tolerance, skill regression, can look from the outside like poor parenting rather than a neurological stress response. The parent who is withdrawn and monosyllabic at the end of a hard week is not disengaging by choice. Their nervous system is in a state of resource emergency.

Consider Aldwyn (name changed), introduced in the Introduction, who did not recognize his autistic burnout until it had been building for over a year. He had been managing his son's PDA profile, navigating a challenging co-parenting relationship, and working part-time throughout a period in which his sensory tolerance progressively reduced, his communication became increasingly effortful, and his capacity for low-demand parenting became less reliable. He attributed all of these changes to stress, a word that acknowledged something was difficult without identifying what specifically was happening. The recognition that what he was experiencing was autistic burnout rather than general stress shifted his response. Stress required him to push through. Burnout required him to reduce load. These are different and opposite responses, and applying the wrong one to burnout makes it worse.

ADHD Dopamine Depletion and the Laziness Misread

Alongside autistic burnout, the ADHD component of the AuDHD parent's profile produces its own specific depletion pattern that is frequently misinterpreted by both the parent and the people around them.

ADHD is fundamentally a disorder of dopaminergic regulation. The dopamine system in ADHD functions differently from neurotypical dopamine systems, producing lower baseline levels of dopaminergic activity and a greater dependence on novelty, urgency, and immediate interest to sustain motivation and engagement (Volkow et al., 2011). In the high-demand, low-novelty conditions of sustained parenting of a PDA child, the ADHD dopamine system is in a structurally unfavorable state: the work is demanding, the feedback is often negative or absent, the routine is high, and the urgency is chronic rather than acute.

Under these conditions, the ADHD adult may experience what looks and feels like motivational failure. The inability to initiate tasks that are clearly necessary. The failure to follow through on plans that were genuinely intended. The flat, gray quality of days when the dopamine system is not producing adequate reward signal to sustain engagement. These experiences are real. They are also not laziness, not lack of care, and not a character flaw. They are the functional output of a dopamine system in a state of chronic under-stimulation and depletion.

The danger for the AuDHD parent is the internalization of the laziness misread. Many ADHD adults carry a lifetime of having their motivational failures attributed to insufficient effort or inadequate character. When the ADHD dopamine depletion arrives in the context of parenting, and particularly in the context of parenting a PDA child where the demands are elevated and the feedback loops are often unrewarding, the old shame story arrives alongside it. The parent who cannot initiate the things they need to do is not failing morally. They are managing a neurological reality with tools that may not currently be adequate to the load they are carrying.

Recognition of ADHD dopamine depletion requires the same shift that recognition of autistic burnout requires: from "I am not trying hard enough" to "my neurological system requires specific conditions to function and those conditions are currently not present."

Compassion Fatigue in the Double-ND Household

Compassion fatigue is a state of emotional and physical exhaustion that results from sustained caring for others who are in significant distress. It was originally described in the context of professional caregivers, nurses, social workers, and therapists, but research has since documented it extensively in parents of children with high medical or behavioral needs (Figley, 2002). In the double-ND household, the conditions that produce compassion fatigue are structurally present: the child's distress is frequent, intense, and genuine; the parent's emotional engagement with the child's distress is high; and the recovery windows between high-intensity interactions are limited.

Compassion fatigue differs from burnout in an important way. Burnout is primarily a depletion of personal resources. Compassion fatigue is specifically the depletion of the capacity to feel and respond to another person's suffering with emotional engagement. The parent experiencing compassion fatigue may notice a reduced ability to feel empathy during meltdown events. They may notice emotional numbness, a going-through-the-motions quality, or even resentment toward the child for the demands being placed. These are not character failures. They are the predictable output of a caregiving system that has been operating at maximum capacity for an extended period without adequate replenishment.

For AuDHD parents, compassion fatigue can be particularly confusing because it may feel like a loss of love, or a sign that they are fundamentally not suited to parenting, or evidence that they are the wrong parent for this child. None of these

interpretations is accurate. The emotional numbness of
compassion fatigue is temporary and responsive to reduced load
and genuine replenishment. It is not a permanent state and it is
not a verdict on the relationship.

Recognizing compassion fatigue requires noticing the specific
quality of the emotional flatness: is it accompanied by physical
exhaustion, reduced sensory tolerance, and skill regression,
which suggests autistic burnout? Or does it have the specific
quality of having run out of empathic response while still having
personal energy, which suggests compassion fatigue more
specifically? Both are valid states. Both require reduced load and
targeted replenishment. The specificity of the recognition helps
identify the specific intervention.

What Sustainable Parenting Actually Looks Like

The phrase sustainable parenting in the context of the double-ND
household requires honest recalibration against what sustainable
actually means for the specific brains and bodies involved.

Standard self-care advice for parents runs toward long baths,
yoga, time alone, and sleep. These are not wrong. They are also
insufficient for the level of depletion being described, and some
of them are inaccessible to ADHD brains that cannot sustain
unstructured rest without activation, or autistic systems that
require specific sensory conditions to experience recovery rather
than mere absence of stimulus.

Genuine self-care for the AuDHD parent is sensory-specific,
cognitively undemanding, and interest-linked. The research on
autistic recovery from burnout has found that the most effective
recovery activities are those that are low-demand, sensory-
appropriate, and connected to genuine interest or comfort rather
than to productivity or social obligation (Raymaker et al., 2020).
For ADHD, the most effective recovery involves novelty,
interest-engagement, and activities that produce genuine

dopaminergic return: the thing you actually find absorbing, not the thing you feel you should find relaxing.

Sustainable parenting also requires honest accounting of what the household's current output capacity is and what it can sustain. Not what it could sustain in an optimal week. Not what it managed in a good month three months ago. What it can reliably sustain right now, with the current level of depletion and the current resources available.

For many double-ND households, sustainable looks like: fewer obligations than a neurotypical household of the same size. More recovery time built in to the week. Lower expectations of what a good enough week contains. More explicit communication between co-parents about state and capacity. More willingness to use external support when it is available and useful.

It also looks like a long-term investment in the specific recovery conditions that work for the specific parent. Not the recovery that is socially legible as self-care. The actual recovery that leaves the parent genuinely more available and more regulated.

Consider Quinlan (name changed), introduced in Chapter 4.0, who had spent two years in a state that she eventually recognized as a combination of compassion fatigue and autistic burnout. Her recovery did not look like the self-care her friends recommended. It looked like two hours alone per week with a specific sensory comfort activity, protected absolutely and non-negotiably. A weekly reduction in social obligations that she had been maintaining out of social norm rather than genuine desire. A decision to stop attending the school events that were sensory-overwhelming and did not directly benefit her son. None of these changes was individually dramatic. Together they produced a measurable shift in her baseline capacity across several months. She describes the period after these changes as the first time in three years that she felt genuinely available to her son rather than performing availability from a place of depletion.

Building a Genuine Support Network

Support network is a phrase that appears in almost every parenting resource and almost never comes with useful guidance about how to build one when you are an AuDHD adult in a social world that was not designed for your communication style, your sensory profile, or the specific demands of your household.

Genuine support for the double-ND household does not primarily look like people who understand PDA in the clinical sense. It looks like people who can be trusted with partial information and will not use it to offer unsolicited advice. People who can be with the parent without requiring social performance. People who provide practical support in a form the parent can actually use. And people who do not make the parent feel worse about their household after the interaction.

This is a shorter list than most people assume. It is also a more useful list. One person who meets all of these criteria is more valuable than ten people who meet one of them.

For many AuDHD adults, the most reliable support network includes other neurodivergent adults, particularly other parents of PDA or demand-sensitive children. The double empathy literature has found that autistic adults consistently report better social understanding, lower social fatigue, and more sustained connection with other autistic adults than in mixed neurotype social contexts (Crompton et al., 2020). Online communities of PDA parents, AuDHD parent groups, and late-diagnosis support networks offer access to this kind of resonant connection without the sensory and social cost of in-person group settings.

Professional support, when it is accessible, should ideally include a therapist with genuine understanding of autistic and ADHD presentations in adults, not just a therapist who treats the surface anxiety without the neurological context. The difference in outcome between generic therapy and neurotype-informed therapy for AuDHD adults is substantial and worth the additional effort required to find appropriate support.

Consider Kenrick (name changed), introduced in Chapter 3.0, who built his support network over approximately eighteen months after a period of near-total isolation during the most intense phase of his daughter's undiagnosed period. His support network is small: a single close friend who has known him for twenty years and requires no social performance; an online community of PDA parents he has never met in person but with whom he has daily contact; a therapist who has her own late autism diagnosis and who understands his communication style without requiring him to code-switch. These three relationships provide more actual support than the much wider social circle he had in his early thirties that required constant management and produced consistent depletion. He does not describe his current network as lonely. He describes it as quiet and reliable.

The Difference Between Recovery and Rest

One of the most useful distinctions for AuDHD parents to make is between recovery and rest, because the two are not the same and confusing them leads to allocating limited time to activities that produce rest without recovery.

Rest is the cessation of effortful activity. Lying down. Watching passive content. Not doing anything requiring significant output. Rest is useful and necessary. It is not sufficient for the level of depletion that autistic burnout and compassion fatigue describe.

Recovery is the restoration of depleted neurological resources through activities that specifically address the kind of depletion present. For autistic burnout, recovery typically involves sensory safety, low social demand, and access to genuine comfort stimuli. For ADHD dopamine depletion, recovery typically involves novelty-engagement, interest-following, and activities that produce genuine reward signal. For compassion fatigue, recovery typically involves relational experiences that are emotionally replenishing rather than demanding: connection with people who require nothing, contact with the natural world, engagement with creative or absorbing activity.

The implication is that identifying what kind of depletion is present is the first step in choosing a recovery activity that will actually work. And that the activity which produces recovery is not necessarily the activity that looks like self-care from the outside. For many AuDHD parents, the activity that genuinely restores neurological resources is one that other people might not recognize as self-care at all: a very specific sensory input, an obscure interest followed without social justification, an hour of complete solitary silence. What matters is the functional outcome, not the cultural legibility.

What Comes Next and What the Book Has Been Building

This chapter is the second to last in the book. Chapter 11.0 is the closing chapter, and it addresses what a genuinely flourishing double-ND household looks like, not as an aspirational ideal, but as a realistic and achievable state that is built over time through the accumulation of small, sustainable changes of the kind described throughout this book.

The foundation that this chapter contributes to that closing chapter is this: sustainable parenting requires honest recognition of the specific depletion patterns that the AuDHD parent experiences, genuine self-care that matches the neurological reality rather than the cultural expectation, and a support network that is small, genuine, and actually supportive. None of these are glamorous. All of them are necessary.

The double-ND household that is still functioning in five years, that contains two people, parent and child, who are both developing rather than simply surviving, will be one where the parent's sustainability was treated as a genuine prerequisite rather than a luxury. Not for the parent's sake alone. For the child's sake. The most important parenting tool in any household is the parent's regulated nervous system. Protecting the conditions for that regulation is not selfishness. It is the job.

Essential Points

AuDHD parental burnout is qualitatively different from neurotypical parental exhaustion. Autistic burnout involves skill regression, sensory sensitivity escalation, and a stealth onset that is often misidentified as general stress. ADHD dopamine depletion produces motivational failure that is neurological in cause and frequently misread as laziness.

Compassion fatigue in the double-ND household is the depletion of empathic response from sustained high-intensity caregiving without adequate recovery. It is temporary, it is responsive to reduced load, and it is not a verdict on the parenting relationship.

Sustainable parenting requires honest accounting of current output capacity rather than aspirational comparison. Genuine self-care for AuDHD parents is sensory-specific, interest-linked, and calibrated to actual neurological recovery needs rather than cultural self-care conventions.

A genuine support network is small, reliable, and actually supportive. One person who meets all of the criteria matters more than ten who meet one. Neurodivergent community, particularly other parents of PDA and demand-sensitive children, provides the kind of resonant understanding that is qualitatively different from neurotypical social support.

Recovery and rest are different. Recovery is the restoration of specific depleted neurological resources. Identifying what kind of depletion is present is the first step in choosing an activity that will actually recover it.

Chapter 11.0 Your Superpower The Neurodivergent Parent Advantage

The Story You Have Been Told

Most of the parenting guidance aimed at neurodivergent adults is built on a deficit model. It describes the challenges, catalogues the shortfalls, and offers compensatory strategies for the things that do not come naturally. Reading enough of it produces a particular internal narrative: you are a parent with extra needs, a parent who requires accommodations, a parent who is managing a harder situation than most with fewer resources than most.

That narrative is not entirely inaccurate. There are genuine challenges to the AuDHD parent profile that this book has not minimized. But it is profoundly incomplete. And the incompleteness matters, because the internal narrative of a parent shapes the quality of their parenting in ways that go well beyond the strategies they deploy.

This final chapter is about what is missing from the deficit account. Not as a motivational corrective, not as false reassurance, but as an accurate description of capabilities that are real, documented, and specific to the AuDHD profile. The parent who is reading this book has spent eleven chapters learning about their challenges with precision. This chapter offers the same precision about their strengths. Both are necessary for an accurate map.

You Understand Demand Avoidance From the Inside

The single most significant advantage an AuDHD parent has in raising a PDA child is one that no amount of professional training can replicate: direct, lived experience of demand avoidance.

Many AuDHD adults, particularly those who received their diagnosis late and in the context of their child's assessment, recognize their own demand sensitivity in PDA descriptions. The visceral response to externally imposed structure. The feeling of a demand arriving in the body as something closer to threat than request. The way compliance becomes harder the more it is insisted upon. The flooding sensation when multiple demands arrive simultaneously. The disproportionate relief when an obligation is cancelled or a deadline moved.

These experiences are not identical to a PDA child's profile. AuDHD demand sensitivity and PDA demand avoidance operate through related but not identical mechanisms. But the experiential overlap is substantial, and it produces a quality of understanding that is qualitatively different from what a neurotypical parent working from the outside of the experience can access.

Research on the role of shared experience in therapeutic alliances has found that therapists and support workers with lived experience of the condition they are supporting demonstrate measurably higher empathic accuracy, better calibrated expectations, and more effective alliance formation with clients than those without lived experience, even when the formally trained professional has significantly more theoretical knowledge (Fardella, 2013). The same principle applies to parenting. A parent who has experienced demand avoidance internally has a baseline calibration for their child's experience that a neurotypical parent reading all the same books cannot acquire from text alone.

This means that when your child cannot comply with something that seems simple from the outside, you have a reference experience. You know it is not stubbornness. You know the compliance is genuinely not available in the way that someone who has only ever read about demand avoidance cannot know it. This knowing is not a small thing. It is the foundation of the specific kind of trust a PDA child needs from their primary adult: the trust that the adult is not misreading the avoidance as willful, not secretly waiting for compliance to reassert itself, not fundamentally confused about what is actually happening. Your lived experience makes that foundation possible.

Pattern Recognition as Parenting Intelligence

AuDHD profiles are associated with a specific kind of perceptual and cognitive capability that is often underdescribed in clinical accounts focused on deficits: a heightened ability to detect patterns, make non-obvious connections, and process sensory and behavioral information in a way that generates insight that neurotypical pattern recognition does not reliably produce.

Research on cognitive strengths in autism has found that autistic people demonstrate significantly enhanced performance on tasks requiring pattern detection, local processing of detail, and identification of regularities within complex information, compared to neurotypical controls (Mottron et al., 2006). In the context of raising a PDA child whose nervous system is highly variable and whose triggers can be subtle, counterintuitive, and context-dependent, this pattern detection capability is not an abstract cognitive strength. It is directly applicable to the most important practical question a PDA parent faces every day: what is happening in this child right now, and what is about to happen next?

The AuDHD parent who has been observing their child for months or years has accumulated a pattern database that informs their responses in ways they may not even be fully conscious of. The slight change in vocal tone that precedes an escalation. The specific sequence of events that reliably predicts a difficult afternoon. The environmental variable, a particular combination of sensory conditions, that accounts for the difference between a manageable day and an unmanageable one. Neurotypical parents can develop similar pattern awareness through sustained observation. AuDHD parents tend to develop it faster, hold it more precisely, and access it more fluidly under the conditions of high-stimulus parenting.

This pattern recognition is a form of parenting intelligence that is rarely named as such. It tends to be attributed to other things: "you know your child so well," "you have good instincts," "you seem to just know when it's going to go wrong." These observations are accurate. But they are describing a cognitive capability, not magic. Naming it as a capability gives you permission to trust it, to act on it earlier, and to communicate it to others (therapists, teachers, co-parents) as the data it actually is rather than as a feeling that might be dismissed.

Consider Bramwell (name changed), introduced in Chapter 7.0, who describes knowing thirty minutes before anyone else in the room that a particular family gathering was going to produce a crisis for his daughter. He could not initially articulate why he knew. Asked to reconstruct it later, he identified seven separate signals he had processed without consciously tracking: a micro-change in his daughter's posture, the volume level of the room at a specific threshold, the number of adults who had directly addressed her in the preceding hour, the length of time since she had last had access to a quiet space, and several more. He was not consciously running through a checklist. He was pattern-matching against years of accumulated observation and producing a reliable prediction. His instinct was data. He had just not previously had a framework for describing it that way.

Justice Sensitivity as Advocacy Fuel

Justice sensitivity, the heightened emotional response to perceived unfairness, is a trait strongly associated with both autism and ADHD and frequently described in clinical contexts as a difficulty to be managed. It produces emotional dysregulation when rules are applied inconsistently, when systems treat similar cases differently, when institutional logic overrides individual need.

This is an accurate description of the challenging dimension of justice sensitivity. It is also an incomplete one. In the context of advocating for a neurodivergent child within educational and healthcare systems that routinely misclassify PDA behavior as behavioral choice, that apply one-size-fits-all frameworks to children whose neurological profiles require individualized responses, and that frequently prioritize institutional convenience over the child's actual need, justice sensitivity is not a liability. It is a propulsive force.

The AuDHD parent with high justice sensitivity in a school meeting where their child's avoidance is being described as deliberate non-compliance is not experiencing an emotion that needs to be suppressed. They are experiencing an accurate recognition that something unfair is happening to their child, combined with a motivational intensity to address it, that gives them energy for advocacy that neurotypical parents in the same meeting often cannot sustain.

Research on justice sensitivity and prosocial behavior has found that individuals with high justice sensitivity demonstrate significantly higher rates of advocacy behavior on behalf of others, particularly in institutional contexts, and that this advocacy is more persistent and less susceptible to social pressure than advocacy motivated by other factors (Schmitt et al., 2010). The AuDHD parent whose justice sensitivity fires in an IEP meeting is not behaving emotionally. They are behaving in the way that the research says produces the most persistent, least easily discouraged advocacy.

The key skill, which this book has addressed in practical form in Chapter 6.0, is channeling that intensity through preparation so that it produces clear, documented, professionally framed advocacy rather than the kind of activation that burns the parent out without producing systemic change. Justice sensitivity is not the problem. Uncontained justice sensitivity is costly. Prepared justice sensitivity is one of the most powerful tools available to any parent navigating institutional systems on behalf of a child who needs them.

Consider Dunstan (name changed), introduced across multiple chapters, who describes his justice sensitivity as the thing that has made him the most effective advocate he could be for his younger child. He has learned to recognize the feeling of injustice in a meeting as a signal to lean into rather than suppress, while using the preparation framework from Chapter 6.0 to ensure the intensity is directed through specific, documented, held-ground responses rather than into a confrontation that satisfies the feeling but does not change the outcome. He describes the combination of his justice sensitivity and his preparation practice as his most effective advocacy tool. The intensity provides the energy. The preparation provides the direction.

Special Interests as Creative Parenting Solutions

The deep interests, sometimes called special interests or areas of intense focus, that are characteristic of both autism and ADHD are frequently described in the context of social cost: the parent who talks about one topic at the expense of other conversation, the time investment that crowds out other activities, the social friction that can arise when the interest does not match the interests of the people around the person who holds it.

These descriptions miss something important. The cognitive depth that an AuDHD adult develops inside a special interest produces a quality of knowledge, creative application, and problem-solving capability that is genuinely unusual. The person who has spent five hundred hours deep inside a subject knows it at a level that a person who has engaged with it conventionally does not, and that depth of knowledge is available for creative application in adjacent domains.

For the parent of a PDA child, special interests are a direct resource for the single most effective PDA intervention available:

interest-based engagement. PDA children are significantly more likely to engage with activities, transitions, and demands that are framed around or connected to their areas of intense interest. A parent whose own interests overlap with the child's has a naturally occurring bridge for this kind of engagement. A parent who does not share the child's interests but has their own deep interests has a model for depth of engagement that they can recognize and respect in the child, and a vocabulary for talking about it.

Special interests are also a source of creative problem-solving that goes beyond the obvious. The parent whose interest is in systems design brings that lens to the household management challenges described in Chapter 3.0. The parent whose interest is in music uses that knowledge to understand the specific sensory profile of sound that affects their child's regulation. The parent whose interest is in narrative or fiction has tools for the indirect communication strategies described in Chapter 5.0. The interest does not need to be directly relevant to PDA parenting to be useful. The cognitive habit of going deep, of following a thread beyond the point where most people stop, of connecting non-obvious information, transfers.

Research on cognitive style in autism has found that the intense focus characteristic of autistic special interests produces measurably greater depth of knowledge acquisition and superior performance on tasks requiring integration of complex information within the interest domain, compared to equivalent time spent by neurotypical individuals (Hermelin, 2001). The depth is real. It is available. And it is transferable.

The Fierce Advocate in the Room

The combination of lived experience, pattern recognition, justice sensitivity, and interest-driven depth produces a particular kind of presence in the rooms where decisions are made about neurodivergent children. The AuDHD parent who arrives prepared, who knows their child's patterns with precision, who has a visceral rather than theoretical understanding of what demand avoidance feels like, and who is motivated by a genuine recognition that something unfair will happen to their child if they do not act, is not a parent who is managing their challenges in a system. They are the most formidable advocate in the room.

Neurotypical parents who advocate effectively for their children do so largely from the outside of the experience. They are relying on information they have acquired, frameworks they have adopted, and emotions they are generating in response to what they understand intellectually. All of that is valid. It is also different in kind from the AuDHD parent who is relying on direct experience, pattern data accumulated over years of close observation, and an emotional response that is built into their neurological architecture rather than constructed situationally.

This does not mean that AuDHD parents are always effective advocates without preparation or support. Chapter 6.0 was explicit about the ways that the same profile that produces advocacy strength also produces specific vulnerabilities in institutional contexts. But the foundation on which that advocacy rests, when it is prepared and channeled, is stronger than the deficit account gives it credit for.

Reframing the Narrative

The work of this chapter, and in a larger sense the work of this whole book, is the work of accurate reframing. Not the positive-thinking version of reframing, where difficulties are relabeled as gifts and challenges are rebranded as strengths. That kind of reframing is not useful because it requires the parent to falsify their experience in order to feel better about it, and the falsification does not hold.

The accurate reframing is more demanding and more durable. It requires holding both the genuine challenges and the genuine capabilities simultaneously, without minimizing either, and constructing a self-narrative that is actually, factually true: I am a parent whose profile produces specific challenges and specific strengths, and the specific strengths are directly relevant to the specific challenges of raising this specific child.

The parent who understands demand avoidance from the inside, who can read their child's patterns before anyone else in the room, who will not stop advocating when institutional systems push back, who brings the cognitive depth of their deep interests to the problem of connection and creative engagement, who is building their household's rhythms with a flexibility that suits both their own neurology and their child's, who is doing the dual healing work of understanding themselves as they understand their child: this parent is not failing. They are doing something that is genuinely hard in a way that is tailored, as if by design, to their particular capabilities.

That is not a small thing to say. It is not easy to hold. On the hard days, when the cascade has happened and the repair is still pending and the burnout is building and the extended family is offering opinions and the school has scheduled another meeting, this reframe is not available. On those days, the Chapter 4.0 safety plan and the Chapter 10.0 recovery practices are the right tools.

But on the other days, the days when something worked because you knew it would before anyone else did, when your child trusted the space you built because you understood from inside why they needed it, when you stood in a meeting and held ground because you knew with a certainty that no one in that room could match what was actually happening to your child, on those days the reframe is not an aspiration. It is a description.

What Comes After This Book

This book has covered eleven chapters of content across the specific intersection of AuDHD parenting and PDA neurology in a child. It has addressed nervous system regulation, low-demand parenting, dual dysregulation, communication, school advocacy, daily life rhythms, late diagnosis grief, relational dynamics, burnout, and now, finally, the strengths that are built into the profile that makes all of this necessary and possible.

The back matter that follows contains practical tools designed for executive-dysfunction-friendly use. They are designed to be usable on the hard days as well as the good ones: short, specific, and accessible without requiring full cognitive function to navigate.

The work continues beyond this book. It continues in the daily practice of the household you are building, in the slow metabolizing of the late diagnosis material, in the ongoing calibration of what sustainable looks like for your specific brain and your specific child, in the relationships you are maintaining and modifying and sometimes ending in service of the household that needs to function.

You already know more about demand avoidance from the inside than any book can teach. You already have the pattern recognition, the justice sensitivity, the interest-driven depth. What this book has offered is a framework for using what you already have, with more precision, more self-compassion, and more trust in the specific capabilities that come with the exact profile you are carrying into the exact household you are raising.

That is what you were built for.

Essential Points

The AuDHD parent's lived experience of demand avoidance provides a quality of understanding of their child's PDA profile that no amount of theoretical knowledge can replicate. It is the foundation of the specific trust a PDA child needs from their primary adult.

Pattern recognition, strongly associated with the AuDHD profile, is directly applicable to the most important practical task of PDA parenting: reading what is happening in the child's nervous system before it becomes a crisis. It is a form of parenting intelligence, not intuition, and it is trustworthy data.

Justice sensitivity, frequently framed as a deficit to be managed, is in the context of institutional advocacy for a PDA child one of the most powerful advocacy fuels available. Prepared and channeled, it produces the most persistent and least easily discouraged advocacy the research describes.

Special interests bring cognitive depth, creative problem-solving, and a model for interest-based engagement that is directly applicable to PDA parenting. The depth is transferable across domains.

Accurate reframing is not the replacement of the difficulty narrative with a strength narrative. It is the simultaneous holding of both: a parent whose profile produces specific challenges and specific capabilities, and whose specific capabilities are directly matched to the specific demands of raising this specific child.

References

- Antshel, K. M., Zhang-James, Y., & Faraone, S. V. (2013). The comorbidity of ADHD and autism spectrum disorder. *Expert Review of Neurotherapeutics, 13*(10), 1117–1128.

- Bal, E., Harden, E., Lamb, D., Van Hecke, A. V., Denver, J. W., & Porges, S. W. (2010). Emotion recognition in children with autism spectrum disorders: Relations to eye gaze and autonomic state. *Journal of Autism and Developmental Disorders, 40*(3), 358–370.

- Barkley, R. A. (1997). Behavioral inhibition, sustained attention, and executive functions: Constructing a unifying theory of ADHD. *Psychological Bulletin, 121*(1), 65–94.

- Barkley, R. A. (2012). *Executive functions: What they are, how they work, and why they evolved.* Guilford Press.

- Barkley, R. A. (Ed.). (2015). *Attention-deficit hyperactivity disorder: A handbook for diagnosis and treatment* (4th ed.). Guilford Press.

- Brown, B. (2010). *The gifts of imperfection: Let go of who you think you're supposed to be and embrace who you are.* Hazelden Publishing.

- Brown, T. E. (2013). *A new understanding of ADHD in children and adults: Executive function impairments.* Routledge.

- Crane, L., Batty, R., Adeyinka, H., Goddard, L., Henry, L. A., & Hill, E. L. (2018). Autism diagnosis in the United Kingdom: Perspectives of autistic adults, parents and professionals. *Journal of Autism and Developmental Disorders, 48*(11), 3761–3772.

- Crompton, C. J., Ropar, D., Evans-Williams, C. V. M., Flynn, E. G., & Fletcher-Watson, S. (2020). Autistic peer-to-peer information transfer is highly effective. *Autism, 24*(7), 1704–1712.

- Díaz-Morales, J. F., & Escribano, C. (2015). Social jetlag, academic achievement and cognitive performance: Understanding gender/sex differences. *Chronobiology International, 32*(6), 822–831.

- Dodson, W. W. (2016, October). Emotional regulation and rejection sensitivity. *Attention*, 8–11.

- Dumont-Mathieu, T., & Fein, D. (2005). Screening for autism in young children: The Modified Checklist for Autism in Toddlers (M-CHAT) and other measures. *Mental Retardation and Developmental Disabilities Research Reviews, 11*(3), 253–262.

- Faraone, S. V., Banaschewski, T., Coghill, D., Zheng, Y., Biederman, J., Bellgrove, M. A., Newcorn, J. H., Gignac, M., Al Saud, N. M., Manor, I., Rohde, L. A., Yang, L., Cortese, S., Almagor, D., Stein, M. A., Albatti, T. H., Aljoudi, H. F., Alqahtani, M. M. J., Asherson, P., ... Wang, Y. (2021). The World Federation of ADHD International Consensus Statement: 208 evidence-based conclusions about the disorder. *Neuroscience and Biobehavioral Reviews, 128*, 789–818.

- Fardella, J. A. (2008). The recovery model: Discourse ethics and the retrieval of the self. *Journal of Medical Humanities, 29*(2), 111–126.

- Figley, C. R. (2002). Compassion fatigue: Psychotherapists' chronic lack of self care. *Journal of Clinical Psychology, 58*(11), 1433–1441.

- Garfinkel, S. N., Tiley, C., O'Keeffe, S., Harrison, N. A., Seth, A. K., & Critchley, H. D. (2016). Discrepancies between dimensions of interoception in autism: Implications for emotion and anxiety. *Biological Psychology, 114*, 117–126.

- Gray, P., Lancy, D. F., & Bjorklund, D. F. (2023). Decline in independent activity as a cause of decline in children's mental well-being: Summary of the evidence. *The Journal of Pediatrics, 260*, Article 113352.

- Green, J., Charman, T., Pickles, A., Wan, M. W., Elsabbagh, M., Slonims, V., Taylor, C., McNally, J., Booth, R., Gliga, T., Jones, E. J. H., Harrop, C., Bedford, R., & Johnson, M. H. (2015). Parent-mediated intervention versus no intervention for infants at high risk of autism: A parallel, single-blind, randomised trial. *The Lancet Psychiatry, 2*(2), 133–140.

- Hagger, M. S., Wood, C., Stiff, C., & Chatzisarantis, N. L. D. (2010). Ego depletion and the strength model of self-control: A meta-analysis. *Psychological Bulletin, 136*(4), 495–525.

- Hermelin, B. (2001). *Bright splinters of the mind: A personal story of research with autistic savants.* Jessica Kingsley Publishers.

- Huang, Y., Arnold, S. R. C., Foley, K.-R., & Trollor, J. N. (2020). Diagnosis of autism in adulthood: A scoping review. *Autism, 24*(6), 1311–1327.

- Iacoboni, M. (2009). Imitation, empathy, and mirror neurons. *Annual Review of Psychology, 60*, 653–670.

- Jachyra, P., Lai, M.-C., Zaheer, J., Fernandes, N., Dale, M., Sawyer, A., & Lunsky, Y. (2022). Suicidal thoughts and behaviours among autistic adults presenting to the psychiatric emergency department: An exploratory chart review. *Journal of Autism and Developmental Disorders, 52*, 2367–2375.

- Leedham, A., Thompson, A. R., Smith, R., & Freeth, M. (2020). "I was exhausted trying to figure it out": The experiences of females receiving an autism diagnosis in middle to late adulthood. *Autism, 24*(1), 135–146.

- Linehan, M. M. (1993). *Cognitive-behavioral treatment of borderline personality disorder*. Guilford Press.

- Meins, E., Fernyhough, C., Wainwright, R., Das Gupta, M., Fradley, E., & Tuckey, M. (2002). Maternal mind-mindedness and attachment security as predictors of theory of mind understanding. *Child Development, 73*(6), 1715–1726.

- Mitchell, P., Sheppard, E., & Cassidy, S. (2021). Autism and the double empathy problem: Implications for development and mental health. *British Journal of Developmental Psychology, 39*(1), 1–18.

- Mottron, L., Dawson, M., Soulières, I., Hubert, B., & Burack, J. (2006). Enhanced perceptual functioning in autism: An update, and eight principles of autistic perception. *Journal of Autism and Developmental Disorders, 36*(1), 27–43.

- Murphy, L. K. (2020). *Declarative language handbook: Using a thoughtful language style to help kids with social learning challenges feel competent, connected, and understood*. Independently published.

- Neff, K. D. (2011). *Self-compassion: Stop beating yourself up and leave insecurity behind*. William Morrow.

- Neff, K. D., & McGehee, P. (2010). Self-compassion and psychological resilience among adolescents and young adults. *Self and Identity, 9*(3), 225–240.

- Newson, E., Le Maréchal, K., & David, C. (2003). Pathological demand avoidance syndrome: A necessary distinction within the pervasive developmental disorders. *Archives of Disease in Childhood, 88*(7), 595–600.

- O'Nions, E., Christie, P., Gould, J., Viding, E., & Happé, F. (2014). Development of the "Extreme Demand Avoidance Questionnaire" (EDA-Q): Preliminary observations on a trait measure for pathological demand avoidance. *Journal of Child Psychology and Psychiatry, 55*(7), 758–768.

- Parham, L. D., Ecker, C., Kuhaneck, H. M., Henry, D. A., & Glennon, T. J. (2007). *Sensory Processing Measure (SPM)*. Western Psychological Services.

- Pfeiffer, B. A., Koenig, K., Kinnealey, M., Sheppard, M., & Henderson, L. (2011). Effectiveness of sensory integration interventions in children with autism spectrum disorders: A pilot study. *American Journal of Occupational Therapy, 65*(1), 76–85.

- Porges, S. W. (2011). *The polyvagal theory: Neurophysiological foundations of emotions, attachment, communication, and self-regulation*. W. W. Norton.

- Raymaker, D. M., Teo, A. R., Steckler, N. A., Lentz, B., Scharer, M., Delos Santos, A., Kapp, S. K., Hunter, M., Joyce, A., & Nicolaidis, C. (2020). "Having all of your internal resources exhausted beyond measure and being left with no clean-up crew": Defining autistic burnout. *Autism in Adulthood, 2*(2), 132–143.

- Schmitt, M., Baumert, A., Gollwitzer, M., & Maes, J. (2010). The Justice Sensitivity Inventory: Factorial validity, location in the personality facet space, demographic pattern, and normative data. *Social Justice Research, 23*(2–3), 211–238.

- Shaw, P., Stringaris, A., Nigg, J., & Leibenluft, E. (2014). Emotion dysregulation in attention deficit hyperactivity disorder. *American Journal of Psychiatry, 171*(3), 276–293.

- Shepherd, D., Landon, J., Taylor, S., & Goedeke, S. (2018). Coping and care-related stress in parents of a child with autism spectrum disorder. *Anxiety, Stress, & Coping, 31*(3), 277–290.

- Siegel, D. J., & Hartzell, M. (2003). *Parenting from the inside out: How a deeper self-understanding can help you raise children who thrive*. Jeremy P. Tarcher.

- Solanto, M. V. (2011). *Cognitive-behavioral therapy for adult ADHD: Targeting executive dysfunction*. Guilford Press.

- Thompson, H. (2019). *The PDA paradox: The highs and lows of my life on a little-known part of the autism spectrum*. Jessica Kingsley Publishers.

- Tick, B., Bolton, P., Happé, F., Rutter, M., & Rijsdijk, F. (2016). Heritability of autism spectrum disorders: A meta-analysis of twin studies. *Journal of Child Psychology and Psychiatry, 57*(5), 585–595.

- Volkow, N. D., Wang, G.-J., Newcorn, J. H., Kollins, S. H., Wigal, T. L., Telang, F., Fowler, J. S., Goldstein, R. Z., Klein, N., Logan, J., Wong, C., & Swanson, J. M. (2011).

Motivation deficit in ADHD is associated with dysfunction of the dopamine reward pathway. *Molecular Psychiatry, 16*(11), 1147–1154.

- Winnicott, D. W. (1953). Transitional objects and transitional phenomena: A study of the first not-me possession. *International Journal of Psycho-Analysis, 34,* 89–97.

- Yehuda, R., & Lehrner, A. (2018). Intergenerational transmission of trauma effects: Putative role of epigenetic mechanisms. *World Psychiatry, 17*(3), 243–257.